Charles
Redd
Monographs
in Western
History

Charles
Redd
Monographs
in Western
History

No. 7
"I'd Rather Be Born Lucky
Than Rich":
The Autobiography
of Robert H. Hinckley

Robert H. Hinckley
and
JoAnn Jacobsen Wells

The Charles Redd Monographs in Western History are made possible by a grant from Charles Redd. This grant served as the basis for the establishment of the Charles Redd Center for Western Studies at Brigham Young University.

Center editor: Thomas G. Alexander
Press editor::   Arnold J. Logie

 Published by
Brigham Young University Press
Provo, Utah 84602

ISBN: 0-8425-0859-7
© 1977 by Brigham Young University Press. All rights reserved
Printed in the United States of America
Additional copies of this monograph or other numbers in this series may be purchased by writing to Brigham Young University, Marketing (University Press), 205 UPB, Provo, Utah 84602.

77 1.5M 27460

To Abrelia Clarissa Seely Hinckley

Robert H. Hinckley at his "Garden of Eden" (Photo by Lynn R. Johnson)

Contents

Acknowledgments	ix
Prologue	xi
1. Politics: The Beginning	1
2. Growing Up in Utah	5
3. Christian Mission	15
4. The Depression	24
5. Federal Relief Programs	39
6. Work Relief vs "Dole"	49
7. Civil Aeronautics	70
8. "Air Conditioning" America	86
9. The War and Sperry	99
10. Postwar Contract Settlement	106
11. Television: Its Freedom	123
12. Political Participation	140
Bibliography	153
Index	155

The authors extend thanks to Sam Weller for his spiritual advice, to Will Fehr for his critique and editorial wisdom, and to Lynn R. Johnson for his photographic work.

Prologue

No doubt you are wondering why I selected for my autobiography the title, "I'd Rather Be Born Lucky Than Rich."

Let me explain by first defining *lucky*. By *lucky* I mean "fortunate." And during my lifetime I have been fortunate—truly fortunate.

I was fortunate in being born to wonderful parents who, although poor financially, were rich in character and integrity. From a pioneer ancestry, they passed on to me physical strength, not only of body, but of mind. They taught me to be responsible yet, at the same time, to be unafraid of new experiences—of pioneering adventures. And they had the wisdom to teach me good work habits. They encouraged learning and provided the example necessary to make me want to learn.

Most important, my parents inspired in me an admiration, respect, and love, not only for my fellowmen, but for one woman, a wife.

Yes, one of the great fortunes of my life was the fact that Mr. and Mrs. John H. Seely decided to send their daughter Abrelia Clarissa to Brigham Young High School, where I met her when I was eighteen. There has definitely been no other influence in my life as important. In fact, her importance cannot be overemphasized. She became a part of my life the day I met her, and she continued to be as long as she was on this earth. Something about that effect was providential. It was more than luck, more than good fortune. Apparently it was meant to be: from no other living soul could I have had the support this woman gave me from the day we met until her departure.

She supported me in every way—encouraging me to seek fulfillment of my dreams, even when this meant more responsibility for her.

Indeed, I was fortunate to have Abrelia for my partner, and we together were fortunate to have great posterity. Our four children are people to be proud of. They have high moral values and the desire to live righteous lives. And they have the ability to cope with life, as difficult as it can appear to them. Their children—my ten grandchildren and eight great-grandchildren, "bright new souls"—have helped me understand change and accept "new ways." In turn, I hope the values I cherish will sift down to them.

Lastly, I have been fortunate in my associates—my friends. Of course they are one of the happiest things about my life because friends are happy things. Without friends I do not know how anyone could accomplish anything. Friends are so important in the way of encouragement, in the way of exchanging ideas and coming up with better ideas. If you appreciate how much friends mean in the development of your life and in the accomplishment of your projects, I believe, you know that there is no other factor as important as friends.

Had it not been for the friends in my life, many of whom were also associates in business and educational projects, I could not have done what I have been given credit for. And I have been given credit for a lot of things that are largely the result of my friends' affectionate interest.

So, you see, during my life I have been more than lucky, more than fortunate. I have been blessed. And believe me, being blessed is worth more than all the money in the world.

Politics: The Beginning

Politics is such a torment that I would advise everyone I love not to mess with it.

—Thomas Jefferson

Although when I was five years old I passed out bills for William Jennings Bryan during his presidential campaign, I was a twenty-three-year-old college student when I took an active part in a political campaign.

After spending three years in Germany as a missionary for the Mormon Church—having been banished by the police from Saxony and Prussia for being a "troublesome foreigner"—I decided it was time to learn more about my government at home.

I was attending Brigham Young University in Provo, Utah, one of the many pioneer communities founded and cultivated by members of The Church of Jesus Christ of Latter-day Saints who fled westward in the late 1840s after being persecuted in New York, Ohio, Illinois, Missouri, and Nebraska because of their religious beliefs and practices.

The first party of Mormon pioneers—143 men, 3 women, 2 children—arrived in the Salt Lake Valley on July 24, 1847. Many more groups of settlers followed and built homes in the valleys of the north-central part of the territory, then called Deseret. In 1850 the site for the city of Provo, some forty-six miles south of Salt Lake City, was selected by Church President Brigham Young to bring together the pioneers who lived in the outlying forts built to protect them from Indians.

Brigham Young University was an outgrowth of Brigham Young Academy, established by Karl G. Maeser in late 1875 under the auspices of Brigham Young, who stated that the beneficiaries of the Academy were to be members in good standing in the church, or children of such members. So in 1914 (eighteen years after the official charter of the Academy was incorporated), most of us enrolled were church members.[1] For this reason, when Heber Jedediah Grant, one of the church's twelve apostles[2] came to address the student body in 1914, everyone had to be present. Those who were absent had to have a good excuse, so I crowded into the school auditorium with faculty members and other students.

Apostle Grant was a tall, thin, austere-looking gentleman who always seemed to stress industry, thrift, and individualism. In the main, I think, he *was* austere: I doubt there was ever any nonsense about the scholarly appearing patriarch. He took his leadership role seriously. Although he may have shared a chuckle now and then with close friends, I couldn't remember ever seeing him laugh, and he had no reason to do so that day as he had come to the school to warn students and faculty alike of the dangers of getting into politics. "It's the stinkingest kind of 'tics there is," he said, banging his fist on the pulpit. "Stay out of it!"

I couldn't believe my ears. He was telling us that politics is "dirty" business, yet he was the son of Jedediah M. Grant, the first mayor of Salt Lake City, and in 1914 he himself was doing all he could to get Reed Smoot reelected to the United States Senate. Grant was alleged to be a Democrat, and Smoot was a Republican. But Smoot, who

---
1. Brigham Young Academy became Brigham Young University in 1903. However, Mormon Church President Heber J. Grant and his counselors didn't decide until 1937 to give the university its stamp as a church school.
2. Like the twelve disciples of Christ, the twelve apostles in the Mormon Church assist the president and his two counselors in leading the masses and preaching the gospel.

had much the same temperament as Grant, was also a Mormon apostle and had already served two terms in the Senate, having been elected by the state legislature (the Constitution did not provide for election of senators by popular vote until 1914).

Although the combination senator-apostle was surely a powerful man in the predominantly Mormon state, my feelings were in accordance with those of many persons in Washington who back in 1903 had opposed Smoot's becoming a senator.

Smoot was appointed an apostle in 1900, three years before he went to the Senate; as a result, his election met bitter opposition in Washington, opposition that lasted more than a year before it was defeated. The specific charge was that when he became an apostle, he took an oath to the Church incompatible with the swearing of allegiance, as a senator, to the national government. Several religious organizations and a number of moral reform associations backed the fight against admission of the Mormon apostle to the Senate.

Smoot conceded that he had asked the consent of the church governing body to become a candidate for the Senate, but he denied that he had been selected as the candidate of the church or that he had taken any oath to it which would supersede his obligation as a senator.

Although a majority of a senate committee reported against seating him, a minority of five recommended he be admitted. Smoot won an early victory with the adoption of a rule requiring a two-thirds majority to expel him. The issue was decided on two ballots. The first to expel was lost 27 to 43; the second, to declare him not entitled to his seat, was defeated 28 to 42.

I was opposed to his reelection to the Senate in 1914 because I believed that high church officials should be high church officials and never get into government. There should be complete separation of church and state.

Obviously neither Smoot nor Grant agreed with me, so I decided right then and there to go out and see just exactly what kind of stinking tics politics really was. I joined the Young Democrats Organization in Utah County and through it began to organize every precinct to get the people in the county out to vote for James H. Moyle, Senator Smoot's opponent in that first senatorial election to be decided by popular vote. Moyle, a long-time Salt Lake City attorney and Mormon Church member (although not an apostle) who had been active in Utah politics since 1889, when he was Salt Lake County Attorney, gave Smoot the closest race he had until his defeat by Elbert D. Thomas in November, 1932. The Utah County vote in that 1914 election was: Smoot, 6,032; Moyle, 5,975.

At the time, my friends accused me of being a Democrat just because my father was a Democrat—which of course was true. But I had also explored the situation for myself and, mindful of the differences between Democrats and Republicans, had decided I was a Democrat because Democrats were for people. Republicans were in favor of things— things like high tariffs to protect business. I mean that they favored property more than people every time.

Father, an ardent Democrat throughout his entire life, a man always mindful of the needs of all citizens, thought my reasoning was sound.

Growing Up in Utah

Fear God, and keep his commandments: for this is the whole duty of man.
—Ecclesiastes 12:13

Mother and Father never missed voting in an election, and both of them usually took part in the local nominating conventions. And they brought me up on the basis that politics is an honorable profession and would always be so long as there were good people in office.

Toward the end of the term of Don B. Colten (a representative from the First Congressional District, 1920-26), Father was importuned to run for the U.S. House of Representatives, but the cost of campaigning and all did not make it practical for him to become a candidate. Father had thirteen children to support.

It was my good luck to be the eldest born of hard-working, but very poor parents. Father, in addition to owning a farm with his brother Lucian, was a geology teacher at Brigham Young Academy in Provo. Though a seemingly notable profession, it was most unprofitable, for he was paid partially in tithing script[3] which could be used only to buy vegetables and produce at church tithing offices. His meager salary went to pay the salaries of his farm employ-

---

3. A tithing script was a piece of paper that represented money and was negotiable at church tithing offices, which were stores generally run by the bishops.

ees and the interest on his farm mortgages.

But with Mother's magical ability to manage what food and funds we had, we were always properly nourished, so I thought we had things as good as anyone else. I didn't know everyone wasn't poor until one day in elementary school when my classmate Annie K. Smoot, daughter of Senator Reed Smoot, brought me an orange—and it wasn't Christmas.

I was born June 8, 1891, in my Grandmother Henry's home in Fillmore, which was made the seat of government in Deseret in 1851, and named after President Millard Fillmore, who made it a territory. Grandmother had been converted to the Mormon religion in England by a missionary named Farr who proposed marriage on the condition that she would get herself to Ogden, Utah. So, Elizabeth Bacon, who subsequently became my Grandmother Henry, left her home in England with her uncle, Dr. William North, and his wife on May 17, 1864, and traveled by sail ship six weeks across the Atlantic Ocean. Then, with a caravan of dedicated church members, she made the wearisome trek across the Plains. Finally she reached Deseret, fulfilling her part of the agreement with Mr. Farr.

But instead of finding rest from her long journey and peace for her soul, she was met with a rude awakening. Brother Farr was already married—not to just one woman, but to several.[4]

So, after a terse "Good day, Brother Farr," the determined young woman started southward, on foot again, not stopping until she reached Fillmore. There friends and distant relatives opened their homes and hearts. And there she met Robert Henry, a devout church member who had come westward with the Mormon Battalion in 1847.

Though many years her senior, he was a good man and an able provider. And most important, he was a widower: he had no wives. So Elizabeth Bacon and Robert Henry

---

4. Polygamy was a common practice among Mormon Church members during this period.

Elizabeth Bacon Henry   Robert Henry

were married. I never knew the grandfather after whom I was named: a breeder of horses of great endurance, he was killed in a horse accident before I was born. But I remember Grandmother as a beautiful and gentle woman whose love and laughter filled my childhood with happiness.

Grandmother had two daughters, Aunt Carrie and my mother, Adeline. Mother, the younger of the two girls, married Edwin Smith Hinckley, son of Ira Nathaniel Hinckley, who in 1867, when he was colonizing Coalville, had been ordered to Cove Creek by Church President Brigham Young to build a fort to protect the settlers from unfriendly Indians. Father was the first child born in Cove Fort. Of course, it wasn't until many years later, when Ira Hinckley moved to Fillmore (where he presided over the Millard Stake of the Mormon Church for twenty-six years), that Father met and married Mother.

When I was a year old, we as a family moved to Ann Arbor, Michigan, so Father could attend the university. To

Adeline Henry Hinckley   Edwin Smith Hinckley

help pay for his schooling, Mother took in Mormon students as boarders, and Richard R. Lyman and John J. McClellan[5] lived with us until Father graduated.

Upon our return home, Father joined the faculty at Brigham Young Academy and moved the family, including Grandmother Henry, from Fillmore to Provo, where Mother ran her new home like a military organization. As soon as each child was old enough, he was given household chores to do before going to school. Mother would inspect each finished job, insisting it be redone until it was done properly.

Father's farm, situated on the banks of Utah Lake, was five or six miles from our home, and every morning and evening when I was in high school, I would ride to the farm to milk the cows. I remember each day after school

---

5. Later Richard R. Lyman was a Mormon Church apostle (1918-43), and John J. McClellan, a famous church organist.

8

Robert H. Hinckley's grandparents, Ira Nathaniel and Adelaide Noble Hinckley

strapping my books to the horse's saddle with the good intention of studying after my work was completed at night. But many times I was so tired that the books never got unstrapped. On weekends I would churn cream to make butter. We had a good reputation for our butter and usually got a few cents more than market rate. But this income, along with Father's small salary, went to pay interest on the farm mortgages.

Though roomy and ample, our first home in Provo had no electricity and no indoor plumbing, so even when the icicles were clinging to the window ledges, we used an outdoor privy. To bathe, we poured hot water from a kettle sizzling on the kitchen stove in a huge washtub. We bathed once a week. Every Saturday, beginning early in the morning, the baths would begin. Because the biggest difficulty was having enough warm water, at times two of us would bathe together, or we would use the same water for

Adeline and Edwin Hinckley and family

different shifts. It didn't matter. We were all clean, at least according to the standards of the day.

As routine as Saturday baths were Sunday church meetings. We would all go to church—Father, Mother and their whole brood, polished and looking as though we belonged. I dreaded Sundays, but despite my pleas, I went to church—always by mother's hand.

When I was five years old, my formal schooling began in the kindergarten of Ida Smoot Dusenberry (she was Senator Reed Smoot's sister and so proud of the fact that she continued using her maiden name) at Brigham Young Academy's training school. Before that, Grandmother Henry, in her gentle but firm way, had taught me more English than I ever could have learned in school. Her method was this: when I would make a mistake conversing with her, she would correct me gently and not dismiss the matter until I had repeated correctly whatever I was saying.

On completion of my primary grades in 1907, I was pro-

Abrelia Clarissa Seely

moted to the Brigham Young High School—where two years later I met Abrelia Clarissa Seely.

Abrelia was from Mt. Pleasant, a town south of Provo that was devoted to farming and livestock raising. She was the daughter of the well-to-do Margaret and John H. Seely—among the world's greatest breeders of livestock. At the time of his death, John H. Seely had the largest herds of registered Shorthorn Cattle and registered Rambouillet Sheep in the world. His sheep were also the most popular because they could be used for both wool and mutton.

Like all livestock men of the day, he was a staunch Republican. Mr. Seely believed the Republicans in government would protect his livestock and thus his income by passing high tariffs. (The Smoot-Hawley Tariff Act, passed in 1930, was one such piece of legislation). For him, Republicanism was a fetish, a religion.

Abrelia was named after two cousins of her parents—one on each side of the family. And although most of her friends in the West called her Abrelia, after we were wed I preferred to call her Clarissa. Of course, she was very attractive, but it was not her beauty that I first noticed. At the beginning of the school year in 1909, President William Howard Taft was visiting Senator Reed Smoot, who resided in Provo. To pay proper respect, the students of the high school were to line up on both sides of the street and cheer as the President and senator rode by. In preparing for the parade all students were gathered in a room, as each was to be given a number. Abrelia was sitting on a table, and because of all the commotion, fell off. That was my first introduction to her. Though quite an informal one, it was the only one we had, and was perhaps one of the luckiest things that ever happened to me. We were both given Number 30, so we marched together from the school and then, on opposite sides of the street, faced each other during the parade.

Soon after, I began walking her home from school as her boarding house was near my home, and I discovered that Abrelia was not only attractive and intelligent, but had a fun-loving spirit that she instilled in everyone else. As our days progressed and as our chats became longer on the corner where our ways divided, we became a matter of neighborhood gossip.

Our friendship was going along just fine until one day I was seen in the pool hall trying to find a friend who today

Margaret Peel Seely   John Henry Seely

would be called a "hustler." He made his spending money hustling up pool games with people he was moderately sure he could beat. Well, the pool hall was off limits to students, and soon President George H. Brimhall and his counselor, my father, were notified of my dereliction. They gave me two choices. I could be ostracized from all social activities, or suspended from school. Neither punishment, I thought, was deserved, because I didn't even know how to play pool, but after discussing the matter with Abrelia, I chose to be suspended from school rather than forfeit the upcoming school dance we had planned to attend together.

    The president and my father were horrified at my decision, and insisted the choice had never been mine. I was to remain in school and not be seen at any social activity. I did as I was told, but suffered little. To their dismay it turned out to be a pleasurable punishment, as Abrelia and I were able to spend more and more time together. Instead of going to dances, we did a lot of visiting, and the longer my banishment went on, the better we liked it. We became such a steady twosome that the lads from Sanpete County began needling me, asking in effect, "Who the hell do you think you are, monopolizing the time of John H. Seely's beautiful daughter?"

While most of the social activities of the day were sponsored either by the school or the church, Provo did have movie houses, but my parents were too poor to give me the 50 cents it cost for two tickets. So, as the end of the school year was nearing and Abrelia was preparing to return to Mt. Pleasant, I announced I would go work in the mines in Eureka to earn enough money to take my girl to a picture show. At the time, I was eighteen.

Within a week or two—very soon after—I received a notice from the church. I had been called on a mission, and in that day a calling was a commandment.

Christian Mission

He who shall introduce into public affairs the principles of a primitive Christianity, will change the face of the world.
—Benjamin Franklin

Naturally I assumed that the Church would meet all expenses, especially since my mission call was to Germany, but I couldn't have been more wrong. The Church, I soon learned, paid only the return fare. My parents, too poor to spare 50 cents so I could take my girl to a picture show, were responsible for all other costs. But without a grumble they began to skimp and save to meet the financial burden, and I realized even more what unselfish, wonderful parents I had.

Of course, they are one of my reasons for saying, "I'd rather be born lucky than rich."

Missionaries in those days were in no way prepared for their calling—at least, I was not. And because of my lack of knowledge about church doctrine in general, I was loath to go. In fact, had it been possible for me to hitchhike home after I arrived in Germany, I certainly would have done so. Again I was lucky. Thomas E. McKay, president of the Swiss-German Mission with headquarters in Zurich, was a tender, understanding man and did all he could to make me feel easy about my dreaded trip abroad. Without his encouragement, things would have been worse than they were.

Robert H. Hinckley while serving as Latter-day Saint missionary in Germany, 1910

I became slightly acquainted with the German government soon after I arrived in Chemnitz, Saxony, my first mission post. There I met up with Lawrence Clayton, a fellow missionary who was working in Leipzig, Saxony, but about to be released. A conference had been called in the mission headquarters in Zurich, so Larry and I started down together, making a sightseeing stop in Munich.

One of the great attractions in Munich was the Royal Brewery, owned and operated by the government. Because it was customary for all tourists to visit, we called at the brewery, only to be informed that it was Peter and Paul's Day, a Catholic holiday recognized by the government, and that the brewery was closed. My German was not good enough at that time for me to be able to follow Larry completely, but he apparently explained to the caretaker that our fathers were brewers in America and we were just passing through and would not be able to return to Munich again.

That seems to be all it took, but it was not until after we had gone on the tour that Larry explained to me how he had made it possible.

That was the beginning of a lasting friendship. A short time later he returned home, and when I next caught up with him, he was associated with the First National Bank of Ogden, Utah, and the Ogden Savings Bank. (The two merged in 1922 to become the Utah National Bank). In his later life he accompanied his boss, Marriner S. Eccles, to Washington, where he served as Eccles's aid. Subsequently, he established his own investment firm in Boston, and later he was appointed a member-governor of the Federal Reserve Board in Washington.

It wasn't long after the brewery incident that I also left Saxony, having been banished by the police who labeled me a "troublesome foreigner" because I was an American missionary. I was warned not to proselyte there again. After Saxony, I spent a short time in Frankfort, and then was put in charge of the church branch in Cologne, where in 1912 I met Eccles, who later also became a close business and political associate. He had been on a mission in Scotland with his cousin Earl Stoddard. Earl's brother, Elmer, was in Germany as a missionary with me, so at the completion of their mission, Earl and Marriner came to Germany to see Elmer.

It was the time of the Mardi Gras in Cologne, so all Mormon missionaries in the outlying areas converged on Cologne to witness the celebration, and as head of the Cologne Branch, I had certain responsibilities to see that everyone was properly housed and so on. Earl came a few days before Marriner. When Marriner finally arrived during the night, he gave my address to a droschen (horse-drawn carriage) driver. When he got to my house, Mrs. Engelhart, my landlady, discovered he couldn't speak any German, so she knew he belonged to me and let him into my room. When we arrived home he was asleep in my bed, which was natural because it was the best of the three beds in the room. I had never seen Marriner before and was a bit indignant that he was in my bed, but Earl said, "Oh, that's just Marriner. He's all right."

"As long as he's in my bed, he's not all right," I replied, taking hold of his feet, while Earl grabbed his head. We lifted him up and dropped him on the floor. Obviously the Lord had work for him to do, because we didn't break his back or skull.

The next time I met up with Marriner, he was president of the Utah National Bank and I was a director of the Mt. Pleasant Commercial and Savings Bank and had been named chairman of the agriculture committee in the state bankers' organization. From then on we met more regularly, particularly after I moved to Ogden in 1927.

After my service in Cologne, I was transfered to Hanover, where I discovered the best way to get a proper bath was to go to the public bath each week. On several occasions I met the American consul, Robert Thompson, and the vice consul, Arthur Bundy, who lived together in a spacious apartment building where the consulate offices were also located.

One week when I went in for my bath, I was not feeling at all well, so after my bath I went into the sweat room where, under supervision, I was properly sweated out and then put to bed to rest until I was dry and able to get out on my own. Consul Thompson found me there and said, "Golly, Bob, you've got a fever. We're going to take you home with us"—which they did. The German couple with whom I was staying were properly notified, but I never moved back with them. The rent was free at the consulate, and the food was better and always sure, so I stayed with Thompson until I was transferred to Berlin, with only three months of my thirty-month mission left.

It was Hyrum Valentine, from Brigham City, Utah, who replaced Brother McKay as mission president and who sent me to Berlin where he said I was to remain until my mission was completed or until the police released me from the country permanently. It was just a matter of which came first.

All American missionaries had difficulty staying for any length of time in Berlin, but by this time I had worn out my American clothing and spoke better German than most. This and the fact that I was discreet in leaving and entering the church enabled me to escape police surveillance. In fact, I was able to extend my mission three more months.

In Berlin I met Emma Lucy Gates, a great Mormon singer who performed in various royal operas in Germany. She told me I should improve my education by becoming a supernumerary in the opera. "I'll fix it up for you," she said, "but if you want to stay on, do whatever they tell you to do. Go to rehearsals whenever they call you, and most important, don't ever pick up your pay. [Extras were given the equivalent of 20 cents a night.] They will appreciate this, and you will always be called."

Lucy Gates was right. I followed her directions explicitly, and the director continued to send me postcards telling me of rehearsal dates. Everything was going along smoothly, and then Emil Gammeter came to town. Gammeter, a church member from Akron, Ohio, was in Berlin on a business trip and sought me out to show him the town. A branch choir practice was scheduled that particular night, but with Gammeter in town I thought I had an excuse not to attend it. However, he insisted on accompanying me to it.

After church meetings, I typically killed an hour or two finishing whatever bookwork there was before walking from the meeting place to catch the bus. This way I could outwait the police. Mr. Gammeter, however, was impatient, so instead of waiting, we went directly to the bus stop after the meeting. Just as I suspected, the plain-clothed policemen were waiting and we were apprehended. The next thing I knew, I was in jail with the city's drunks. I was searched, and in my pocket the police found a Rohr Postcard (sent by pneumatic tube to areas adjacent to Berlin) from the opera director demanding I appear at an upcoming rehearsal. Unlike my church mail, which was sent to "Robert Henry" at the chapel, this was addressed to "Robert H. Hinckley," so the police charged me with being deceitful in having two names. I explained that Henry was my mother's name and that instead of using a hyphen between my two names, as the Germans did, I simply used my middle name. My explanation seemed to satisfy them, but nevertheless, I spent the night in jail.

The next morning I went before the chief of detectives, who restored my belongings and told me to take my time in leaving the country—but leave. "Just don't show up around the church while you are here," he said. "And if you ever get back to Germany, come and see me." We corresponded for a while after my mission.

Somehow I had managed to get Emil Gammeter off, and he was free to establish his agency in Berlin. I didn't see him again until he moved to Monticello, Utah, and became a member of the state legislature from that area.

When I returned home from my mission that fall, my girl, Abrelia Seely, was still waiting for me, but our marriage plans had to be delayed two years while I paid off missionary debts. In 1913 I enrolled in Brigham Young University, where my former teacher of German and friend, James L. Barker, gave me a job teaching two classes of college German. Though it was unusual for a student to teach, my German was excellent, and Professor Barker said he never had a better German teacher on his staff. I also earned money to attend school by working for Utah Power and Light Company, which at that time didn't have a system of collecting bills. If a customer didn't pay at the proper time, his power was disconnected. Ambrose Merrill, the company's manager in Provo, was a good businessman and realized that disconnecting customers' power was no way to win friends, so he told me to set up a collection system, which I did merely by sending out letters, notifying customers of unpaid bills. That way no one could say, "You cut off my lights without telling me."

Finally, in 1915, after working two jobs for two years, my debts were nearly paid off, and I wrote a letter to John H. Seely requesting a meeting regarding my marriage proposal to his daughter. So he would have no doubts about my background, I wrote the letter on stationery of the Young Democrats Organization, of which I was an officer. Doing so was not altogether bright, but at least it was honest.

I received no reply, but then Abrelia had told me not to expect one. She said her father had received my letter, and if I would come down to Mt. Pleasant, she would guarantee he would see me. I made the journey, and one day I followed him into the garden, telling him what I had in mind. He listened with no comment, until I was through speaking. Then he gave me a quizzical look, which I later learned was a twinkle of his own when he was enjoying something, and he said, "Well, I don't have to live with you."

That was that: Mr. Seely continued to be a staunch Republican, and I a staunch Democrat, but we became close friends. In fact, I never had a better friend. Abrelia and I were married June 23, 1915, in the Salt Lake Mormon

Temple. She too was a Republican, and from that time we on we talked issues always, but I never asked her how she voted or persuaded her how to vote. Gradually, however, she became a Democrat, and a funny incident arose out of it.

In 1928, when Al Smith, a Democrat, was opposing Herbert Hoover, a Republican, for President of the United States, Abrelia's brothers came up from Mt. Pleasant to tell her to vote for Hoover. In their opinion, if a Democrat was elected the country would go to hell, which meant they would lose their sheep, and that meant the family estate. Abrelia and I had just attended a meeting of the Socialist Party in Ogden, where Norman Thomas, also a presidential candidate, spoke. We were both impressed with his greatness, so unknown to me, Abrelia told her brothers—to their horror—that she was going to vote for Norman Thomas. She didn't, of course, and neither did she vote for Hoover, but he was elected. In spite of their victory, however, in the market crash of 1929, the Seelys still lost their sheep and practically all the property they had inherited from their great father.

The fall after Abrelia and I were married, I began my senior year at Brigham Young University, and on account of Abrelia, it was the most successful year scholastically and in every other way. Because of her encouragement I had been able to complete one year of high school and four years of college in three years, and upon graduation, I moved with my wife from the family home at 320 N. 2nd East, Provo, to Mt. Pleasant, where I had signed a contract to teach at the North Sanpete High School for $1,100 a year.

The wedding of Robert H. Hinckley and Abrelia Clarissa Seely, June 23, 1915

The Depression

Politics is the practical exercise of self-government and somebody must attend to it if we are to have self-government.
—Elihu Root

In Mt. Pleasant we took up residency with Abrelia's parents as she was the last child at home and Mrs. Seely was in poor health. I, in addition to assuming my teaching position at North Sanpete, opened an automobile dealership to earn enough money to study law.

Since I was a child I had wanted to become a lawyer. And I had some reason to do so: the best lawyers in Utah at that time were from both sides of my family—Will and Paul Ray on Father's side, Will and Sam King on Mother's side. But I knew I hadn't a prayer of following in their footsteps unless I got some money, so in 1915 I established the Seely-Hinckley Automobile Company with my brother-in-law, Leonard. There was one problem. I was a professor's son, and no one had told me that when you go into business you have got to put money back into the business to make money. When I got ready to make an early break and go to law school, Leonard refused to buy my share of the business even though I offered him a price at a loss to me. Nor would he sell his share at the price I had offered to sell out to him, so in coming up with a much bigger ante to buy him out, I was unable to afford law school. And I have been in the automobile business ever since—sixty years to be exact.

When we first opened the business, as the first automobile dealers in Sanpete County, I became salesman, mechanic, bookkeeper, general manager, telephone operator, distributor, and promoter of Dorts, an auto manufactured by a contemporary of William C. Durrant, who was responsible for developing General Motors, Incorporated. It was not long, however, until other factory representatives were calling on us to take their lines, which cost us nothing outside a demonstrator. Each automobile company usually had a stock in Salt Lake City, so every time we sold a car, I could go to Salt Lake to pick it up. Besides Dorts, we sold Hudsons, Nashes, Buicks, and finally Dodges. I accepted the Dodge as an associate dealer under the Botterill Dealership in Salt Lake City, and served in this capacity for many years until I was made a direct dealer—the only one in Southern Utah—by the Dodge Company.

It was during this time that I became acquainted with Hugh Ferry, treasurer of Packard Automobile Company, later to serve as its president until Packard merged with Studebaker. Reginald Fry, owner of the Salt Lake Dodge dealership and a former officer of Dodge Brothers Corporation, had invited Ferry and others to visit Utah from Detroit. Because Fry was a newcomer to Utah and didn't have any ideas of how to entertain them, he asked if I would come up from Mt. Pleasant. I suggested a trip to Mt. Timpanogos, between Provo and American Fork Canyons, and made all the arrangements for a horseback ride to the top. We started to ride from Pleasant Grove on mountain climbing horses, and were doing really well until one of the riders, the head of the Alemite Company (Alemite was a method used to lubricate cars in that day) began to lean more and more toward the mountain as we rode up the steep mountainside. He thought that manner was much safer because on his other side he could see down into the deep canyon below.

As he leaned toward the mountain, the horse moved the other way to maintain its equilibrium, and as a consequence, the saddle slipped and this poor man was hanging onto the saddle for dear life. Ferry called the man by name and said, "What the hell are you trying to do down there, alemite that horse?"

Of course, from then on I remembered Hugh Ferry in all circumstances. After that, Ferry and two of his friends, a doctor and a broker, would put a little money in the kitty at the beginning of each year, and the broker would invest it. When it came vacation time they would spend whatever the kitty had earned. Usually they did quite well, and on several occasions they passed through Ogden on the train while vacationing. They would always invite me to come down, and when I arrived, there was always a bar set up in the drawing room. I returned their hospitality on one occasion by taking them across the street to a hotel operated by Sam Morari for sheep herders. He had bootleg whiskey and a room where Ogden's tired businessmen could come and enjoy it. That day my friends made the most of it; they were practically drinking with both hands. Later Morari said he had never seen such hearty drinkers and he thought more of his whiskey after that encounter than he ever had before.

It was on this occasion that I almost accompanied my friends on their vacation. When we finished at Mr. Morari's, they insisted I board the train with them, and I was unable to get off when the train started. By the time we got the conductor to come to a halt, the train was out to the city limits, and I had to walk back.

Ferry was the man who later got me involved in the Question Club, of which another dear friend of mine, Tex Colbert, later became a member. Tex belonged to a New York law firm that represented Chrysler Corporation, and while Walter Chrysler was alive he asked that Tex be brought to Detroit and made house counsel. Colbert later was pushed into the manufacturing and production business when Dodge, a Chrysler subsidiary, was called upon during the war to build Curtiss-Wright airplane engines. Their plant was established in Chicago. Well, at the outset people said he would never achieve the accuracy or quality of Wright-built engines, but according to government inspectors, he not only did that, but also produced engines for less cost to the government than they had been paying the original manufacturers. This endeavor put him into prominence as a manufacturer, and at the end of the war he became the head of the Dodge division of Chrysler—later, in the normal sequence of things, to become president of Chrysler.

Even though when we first opened the automobile dealership we had no competition from other car dealers in Sanpete County, we sold few cars because the roads were still dirt paths with many ruts and curves that followed section farm lines. Furthermore, cars couldn't be used in the winter and had to be stored in barns on four blocks of wood. So, while there were people who could afford to buy, say, an open-top Dodge Touring Car (for $800), few wanted one because most insisted "The old horse and buggy is good enough for me." We had another problem. When we did sell a car, we had to teach every member of the family to drive as there were no laws regulating driving age. This was never easy.

The North Sanpete School Board had employed me to teach two years of German and social studies (civics and history) in North Sanpete High School, which I thought was a bit foolish, because they offered only one year of agriculture at the rural school. So, upon my arrival I convinced the board that because 100 percent of the students were brought up on farms, the emphasis should be reversed. On the basis of my recommendation, I wound up teaching one year of German and one year of agriculture. I was also made football coach, and despite my inexperience—I had never played a game of college football—the team became the champions of southern Utah.

While I was teaching in the high school, a war was in progress in Europe. In 1914 Austria-Hungary declared war on Serbia; Germany declared war on Russia; France invaded Belgium; Great Britain declared war on Germany. As time went on, it became more and more apparent that the U.S. too would be entering the European war, so participating in politics became part of everything I taught in my social studies class. I emphasized the responsibility of citizenship and the responsibility of all citizens to participate in their government by doing whatever they could through their political parties to make local, state, and national governments better. I admonished the students to go home and, putting it bluntly, "to work their parents over" to get them involved.

My students followed my advice, and in 1918 I became a victim of my own classroom lectures.

That year the area was hit with an epidemic of virulent influenza—something that had never happened before. Many died because there were not enough doctors to make rounds. We who were not affected helped others as best we could. When a family member was stricken, he was isolated from other family members, of course, and that family would limit its circulation as much as possible and still carry on.

Public meetings indoors were banned, so the Democratic Convention was held in the grandstands at the county fair grounds in Manti. I was teaching school at the time and couldn't attend, but my absence didn't seem to matter. My students' parents nominated me, and I, a Democrat in an overwhelmingly Republican county, was elected a representative from Sanpete County.

The regular term of the Utah Legislature was sixty days, and legislators were paid $4 a day, plus travel expenses for one trip to Salt Lake City, so Abrelia, our son Robert, and I moved into the Hotel Utah, where legislators were given a special rate. Throughout that session I was known as the "baby" of the legislature because of my youth, and I soon drew attention to my liberal views when I voted against the anticigarette bill, which became law in the next legislative session but was subsequently repealed because of its unpopularity.

After that one term we traveled back to Mt. Pleasant, and I began teaching again. However, not for long.

In 1920 I was hunting deer in the Kaibab Forest with some friends and missed another convention. The Mt. Pleasant Democrats said they waited as long as they could for my return and then went ahead, without my permission, and filed a ticket with me as candidate for mayor. When I heard the news I was very much out of patience, to say the least, and called together the group that had done the dirty deed and told them I was going to resign. With less than one week until the election, they said I could resign if I wished, but I would just make a fool of myself. A Democrat hadn't been elected since no one could remember. Besides, I didn't have whiskers, and you had to have whiskers to win. My Republican opponent, Abrelia's Uncle Joe, had a most handsome mustache. With this assurance, I remained in the race.

The day before the election, Uncle Joe set out to visit every member of the very large Seely family to tell them, among other things, that Rob was a very nice boy and if any of them wanted to vote for him, it was all right. That is how sure Uncle Joe was of being elected. I had done nothing and had no time to do anything in the way of campaigning, but with Uncle Joe's help, I was elected by sixteen votes. I am sorry to say he didn't speak to me for the next two years, while I was mayor.

While mayor, I continued operating my automobile business. In fact, it kept us in Mt. Pleasant until 1927, when the Dodge dealership in Ogden, Utah, a much larger operation than my own, became available. With the financial help of my old missionary friend, Dean Brimhall, I purchased the Ogden dealership from Walker Cheeseman, and in the summer of 1927 I moved the family north. By this time Abrelia and I had four beautiful children—Robert Henry Jr., Elizabeth (Betty), John Seely, and Paul Ray. One of my good friends and employees, John Clift, ran the business in Mt. Pleasant for me until just before the market crash of 1929, when I closed out. This didn't stop our progress in the automobile business, however. In 1954 I gained other interests.

This came about when George Eccles, Marriner's brother and president of First Security Bank Corporation, asked me if I would like to buy the real estate at 2309 S. State, Salt Lake City, which had been mortgaged to the bank by a Dodge dealer named Les Taylor. After some discussion, the land was purchased and Taylor became my tenant—I thought for an indefinite period. But Taylor, who had sold the property to bail himself out, was soon out of money again, so I received another call from Eccles. This time he asked me if I would like to buy the dealer operation. I said no.

Eccles persisted and said if I didn't buy it, he was going to buy it and get my son John, who had taken over the Ogden dealership in 1948, to go into business with him. I thought that a lot of nonsense, but George was nevertheless serious, so I bought Taylor's operation, and John ran the dealerships in both Ogden and Salt Lake City.

The Salt Lake dealership opened on my birthday, June 8, 1955, and that night we had a banquet at the Hotel Utah that was attended by all the factory officials along with local dignitaries. During dinner John got a call from the commercial office of the Commercial Credit Corporation in Salt Lake City, telling him that the Dodge dealer in Logan, Utah, to whom we distributed cars, was out of trust and that they were taking over his entire inventory, which we found out later we owned. So, in the middle of the dinner, John had to dispatch our certified public accountant, William Stockdale, to Logan to retrieve the cars before we lost our shirts.

My eldest son, Robert, came into the business in 1955 from an entirely different environment; he had been flying six-engine jet bombers out of Roswell, New Mexico, in the Strategic Air Command. He came home that July, and he and John immediately began to commute daily from Ogden to Salt Lake City so that Robert could become oriented with the Salt Lake City dealership. For my sons there were trying experiences, and at times it must have appeared that everyone was standing around waiting to see what would happen. But they stood fast together during the formative years and finally pulled the address, 2309 S. State, into a business. Robert moved with his family to Salt Lake City in September, 1955, and the automobile business gradually fell into a pattern.

Then, on November 11, 1957, the boys signed an agreement with Chrysler for a Dodge truck-center franchise, putting them in the business of distributing Dodge trucks throughout a three-state area. This wholesale franchise was combined with the automobile business facilities, and things began to be done on a minimal-expense basis to cover the overhead. But the truck franchise brought in some additional revenue on the return from the factory base when they wholesaled Dodge trucks to dealers, and soon the dealership became more and more competitive. With competition, however, came the real headaches.

The Gledhill Dodge dealership in downtown Salt Lake City was lobbying very diligently to cancel any other Dodge dealership in the metropolitan Salt Lake area, and in 1964 Hinckley Dodge was threatened with cancellation. They tried to move Robert south to the small community of Murray, but he didn't like that, so in leaving one of the negotiation meetings, I said to the factory representative who was considering our cancellation, "Why don't you sometime give us the opportunity to move to Salt Lake City proper?" Nothing came of this until 1965, when Robert was asked if he would like to buy Gledhill Dodge at 1000 S. Main Street. The only problem was that the question came to Robert after the factory had sought to merchandise the dealership on a formulative basis to anybody else that was interested—two days before Gledhill was to be bought out. So John, Robert, and I met, and it was the consensus that we had to go. We had to do this whether it was an act we thought monetarily prudent or not, because if you weren't growing, you were getting littler. So, on August 31, 1965, Robert moved in and took Gledhill out of 1000 S. Main Street—keeping Gledhill's promise that there would be only one dealership in metropolitan Salt Lake City.

To Robert, this was more or less like starting over—like poking a hole in the boat to find the water and finding only that the water keeps running in. He had divided the two functions—the truck dealership at South State and the car dealership on Main Street—which almost doubled his overhead again. But soon the new address was recultivated; in three to four years it went its full cycle, and the automobile business—which had grown from Mt. Pleasant to Ogden to Salt Lake City—became a profitable venture for my sons.

In 1927, the year that Dean and I became partners in the Ogden Dodge dealership with the backing of Archie Bigelow, president of the Ogden State Bank, we also began the Utah-Pacific Airways Aviation Company, a fixed-base operation. We became a dealership for planes, employed a pilot, and sold plane rides and flight training. But because the aviation business, like the automobile business, was a pioneering adventure, we had to cope with another argument when selling plane rides. People would say, "I'll fly as long as I can keep one foot on the ground."

Despite this lack of enthusiasm, I was unafraid in my new pioneering adventure. Praise the Lord for my parents, who were pioneers and taught me, "Nothing ventured, nothing gained."

Our company, the largest operation in the Rocky Mountain states, first represented the Beechcraft organization and later became distributor for Curtiss-Wright Company. We promoted the first aviation census of big game, and our method proved so successful that it immediately supplanted the inefficient and expensive ground counting. This work was done in cooperation with the U.S. Biological Survey for the Yellowstone Park area and for the State of Wyoming. Under our direction, too, the first experiments in the use of airplanes for controlling forest fires were made for the United States Forest Service. An entire summer was used in devising methods for dropping supplies and men to control forest fires in remote areas.

While Abrelia and I were searching for a home in Ogden in 1927, the family lived in a house we rented from Jake Parker in an attractive spot in Ogden Canyon. The house had a porch that became a great playing place for little Paul, who threw everything, including his mother's corsets, over the porch railing into the river. Though Robert made many attempts to rescue the items, there were many things (like the silver napkin rings we had started to collect on our honeymoon in Yellowstone Park) that he couldn't retrieve because they were too small to find.

During the time the family lived in the canyon home—before we finally located a suitable home at 2560 Jefferson Ave., a famous old residential street—I rented a room in the newly constructed Bigelow Hotel so I could be closer to the downtown dealership in Ogden. I was the first tenant in the hotel, named after Archie Bigelow. In the market crash of 1929, the hotel's name was changed to the Ben Lomond Hotel as the management decided it wasn't a good idea to name a hotel after Mr. Bigelow, whose bank, like thousands of others, had failed.

The Hoover Administration had hardly begun when, in 1929, the country suffered the worst business crash in its history. The stock market crashed that fall and at the end of the year the government estimated the crash had cost investors billions of dollars. After the crash the country sank steadily into the most severe depression in history. Millions lost everything they owned. Banks failed, factories shut their doors, businesses were paralyzed. Everybody was hit. By the end of 1930 more than six million Americans were out of work. A year later, that number doubled.

As conditions started to go from bad to worse, a group of thinking businessmen in the Ogden area began meeting monthly or bimonthly to discuss what was wrong with the country—why there was such great unemployment in this land of plenty. Initially, we called ourselves "The Friedenkers" to signify the free-thinking atmosphere of our meetings, but eventually we had to drop the name because the town residents changed it to "Free Drinkers".

Besides me, those who met regularly were Dean Brimhall; Abe L. Glasmann, publisher of the Ogden *Standard Examiner*; Paul Thatcher, a lawyer; Darrell J. Greenwell, editorial writer at the *Standard*; Bill Bowman, reporter; and Billy Meal, an outdoorsman and superintendent of one of the famous duck clubs at Willard Bay. Marriner Eccles, who was then president of First Security Bank Corporation, was also a frequent visitor at the meetings, particularly after he had done his homework as no other banker had in examining the wrongs of the land and had developed a Five Point Plan. We tried to get that plan presented to Congress through hearings of the Senate Finance Committee, which was chaired by Utah Senator Reed Smoot. Efforts had been made to get Smoot to invite Marriner to Washington. But for some reason he would not respond.

Unusual as it was for a state as small as Utah to have two senators on such an important committee, Utah Senator William H. King was nevertheless also a member. King was my mother's cousin, so I asked him to invite Marriner to make his presentation, which he did.

In February 1933, a few weeks before Marriner was scheduled to appear before the committee, he attended a luncheon that I was coordinating at the Hotel Utah in Salt Lake City, in which Stuart Chase, a writer and lecturer on economics, was to be the guest speaker. I had been appointed a member of the Board of Regents of the University of Utah in 1929 by Governor George H. Dern, a fellow Democrat and good friend and, as a regent, I was made Chase's host while he was in town. I invited Marriner to be my guest.

Chase's train was delayed by a snowstorm, and he arrived in Ogden at about the time the luncheon was to begin. Because he had to be driven to Salt Lake, he was unable to arrive on schedule, so I asked Marriner to come out of the audience and express his views on the current economic dilemma until Chase arrived. After Marriner had spoken for about twenty minutes, Chase appeared and took the stand. But because he had had no time to eat his lunch, I invited him to adjourn to another dining room following his lecture. And I also asked Marriner to join us, giving him a chance to continue his discussion. Chase was impressed with Marriner's plan for recovery, and suggested he visit Rex Tugwell (one of President Franklin D. Roosevelt's brain trusters) in New York City following his appearance before the Finance Committee in Washington.

As a result of meeting Chase and of his appearance before the committee, Marriner later became assistant secretary of the treasury and then was appointed by President Roosevelt as a member of the Federal Reserve Board, later to serve as chairman, distinguishing himself during the troublesome times that followed.

As members of "The Friedenkers" became involved in business and political endeavors out of the area, the group naturally dissolved, but my close association with these men continued. I borrowed Darrell J. Greenwell from the *Standard* to work for the Works Progress Administration later during the depression years. In October 1945 Abe Glasmann and his son-in-law, George Hatch, and I would organize KALL Radio in Salt Lake City.

As the depression continued, money became the scarcest thing there was. Jobs were so few that in Weber County the school board passed a ruling that married women could not teach. But because they were in such desperate need of money, some female teachers got married anyway, and did not let the board know about it until the school year was completed. To put an end to this trickery, the Park City Board of Education added a clause to its teaching contracts that if a woman was secretly married during the school year, when her marriage became known, the board would sue her for every cent she earned after her marriage. Single men were also discharged from jobs in order to let the married men work.

Many people who lived in the cities were forced to move into the country with relatives as they had no money for house payments. Farmers who bought potato seed, planted, watered, cultivated, and harvested their produce received only 30 cents for 100 pounds of potatoes. Parents bought their children clothes that were far too large as they feared they would not be able to afford others but knew that their children would grow into them.

I heard a story of one man in such despair that he walked into an Ogden grocery store and in front of everyone there picked up a 50 pound sack of flour and walked out of the store without paying for it. The store owner, instead of calling the police, followed him home, arriving just in time to see the man set the flour on the table, while his starving children frantically tore the sack open and began eating the flour with their hands.

With times this hard, it looked as if Dean and I would go under in both businesses, so we decided the best thing to do would be for him to take the aviation business and see if he could pull it through, and I would take the car dealership. Utah-Pacific Airways survived, and thanks to T.E. Thomas, known to most of us as "Tommy," I was also lucky enough to pull through.

Tommy, the liquidator of the Ogden State Bank, called me one day and said, "Bob, I am sorry, but I am going to have to take over your automobile company."

I replied, "Why has it taken you so long?" I obviously knew better than he that I was bankrupt. But later when I met with him in the bank office, I suggested that inasmuch as I knew more about the automobile business than he, if I would be permitted to manage it, I might be able to pull it out.

Of course, with the understanding that he would be informed of what went on daily, he agreed to this, but only after he asked me what my salary was, and I told him "nothing." He also asked me about other organizational matters, including how much rent I paid, and to whom. I told him that I paid $250 a month to John Rushmer, an optometrist whose offices were less than a block away.

"Well," Thomas said, "let me see what I can do," and he left the office. On his return from visiting Rushmer, he said, "The best I could do was $40." I thought he meant he had gotten $40 taken off the $250, but that was not the case. He had gotten Rushmer to reduce the rate from $250 to $40. That was a great start, and from there things only got better. It was with the help and guidance of another friend, E. G. Bennett of First Security Bank Corporation, that I was able to liquidate my indebtedness to the Ogden State Bank entirely.

However, throughout these difficult times, any money I was fortunate enough to get went to pay the help and any other bills that came in. The staff was reduced and salaries cut to the bone, but my two remaining employees on the payroll, W. C. Beadles and Edna Murray, were willing to wait until we had funds to pay them. Few cars were sold because few were able to purchase them. On some unpaid bills, I developed a system of taking in produce, fresh vegetables, and meat from farmers who had no money. Although this is what the family lived on, I doubt the children remember it as much of a hardship. We lived well even though we had no money. Dear Mrs. Hinckley saw to it that her children were happy, had clean clothes (though sometimes a bit patched), and were never hungry. It was surprising how many ways she could cook up beans and sow belly and make them like it. We had chili regularly (with a lot of beans and little meat), and quite often, in spite of the boys' dislike for the dish, our house lady, Bessie S. Fretz, would make cheese souffle. More than once, Paul drew her attention while John swiped the double boiler off the stove. But their mother insisted they eat it anyway.

All during the Depression Mrs. Hinckley also insisted that Betty continue with her piano lessons. When Betty didn't practice as she should, the teacher would get short with her and say it was unfortunate she didn't try harder, for Abrelia, who paid only when she could, said she would scrub floors if necessary for Betty to continue.

The Depression went on and on, and when the federal government refused to offer any assistance, Governor Dern stepped in to help solve the problem. In 1931 he established the Volunteer Relief Committee and appointed both Marriner Eccles and me as members.

Federal Relief Programs

I have never liked poverty. I have never believed that with our capitalistic system people have to be poor. I think it is an outrage that we should permit hundreds and hundreds of thousands of people to be ill clad, to live in miserable homes, not to have enough to eat, not to be able to send their children to school for the only reason that they are poor. I don't believe ever again in America are we going to permit the things to happen that have happened in the past to people.

—Harry Hopkins

I first met George H. Dern when he was a senator from Salt Lake County in the Utah State Legislature, having been elected in 1914 on the Democratic-Progressive fusion ticket. We became good friends, and whenever he was in Mt. Pleasant he was a welcome overnight guest at our home.

It was during his second term as governor (he was first elected in 1924 and reelected in 1928 by the largest vote ever given to any candidate in the state, winning by a majority of over 30,000—although the Republican national ticket with Herbert Hoover for President carried the state) that he organized the Volunteer Relief Committee to take care of the relief problems in the state.

At the beginning of the market crash in '29, President Hoover said, "The fundamental business of the country ... is on a sound and prosperous basis." From then on he did very little to recognize or deal with the depression that was getting underway. As private charities and breadlines were swamped, he bravely predicted that unemployment would pass its peak in the next sixty days. When it didn't, he refused to allot any federal food or cash for direct relief of the unemployed, because that would be a "dole." He assured the people that the same private enterprise that made the crash would eventually cure it. All he would do was loan federal money to business firms, and through the Reconstruction Finance Corporation he allocated $2 billion for helping hard pressed banks, factories, and railroads.

Utah, like all the other states, was forced to use state funds for relief, and those were limited.

Dern had become friends with Governor Franklin D. Roosevelt of New York State, and in fact had an agreement with Roosevelt that should he be elected president, Dern would be made secretary of the interior. Roosevelt's own philosophy had differed from Hoover's in that he believed that the government had a "definite obligation to prevent the starvation or dire waste" of its people "who try to maintain themselves, but can't." And, in his own state he had established a Temporary Emergency Relief Administration—the first of its kind to do the job.

Roosevelt, whose presidential campaign in 1932 was directed by James A. Farley, Democratic Party chairman in New York State, outlined a program to meet the economic problems of the nation. He pledged a new deal if elected—a program to lead the "forgotten man" out of depression.

During the election campaign Roosevelt visited thirty-eight states, showing the voters he was physically able to be President. He promised to provide relief for the unemployed, to help the farmers, and to balance the budget.

In the election Roosevelt received 472 electoral votes to only 59 for Hoover. On March 4, 1933, he was inaugurated, and throughout the streets people sang "Happy Days Are Here Again" to celebrate his victory.

As promised, once Roosevelt was elected, Dern's position as secretary of the interior was announced. But California complained about the appointment. Earlier Utah had sided with Arizona and refused to be part of a six-state compact over the use of the waters of the Colorado River. For years Governor Dern held out so as to give Arizona a chance to work out her differences with California and come into the compact. His position was that Arizona had certain rights as a state which could not be violated by the Federal Government or by other states. As a result of this, California raised such a fuss over Dern's appointment that Roosevelt was forced to change his mind to pacify the state. He appointed Harold L. Ickes as secretary of the interior and Dern as secretary of war. Nothing could have been more distasteful to Dern, who was a peace-loving man. He died in office, and I have always felt that his position as head of the War Department could have contributed to his early death.

After Roosevelt was elected, federal road funds were made available for relief, with the understanding that they would be paid back. The funds were allocated on the basis of federal domain within the state, and because Utah was a land grant state, with some 70 percent of the total area federally owned, we received a high percentage of road funds. Wyoming also would have received a goodly amount because the state was high in federal land acreage, but the state decided not to take any of the funds.

Eccles and I concluded that there would be no future recall of these funds and established for the committee the policy of taking all the road funds available and using them for direct relief purposes, which we did. Consequently our people were taken care of up to that point. Our judgment was right; the money was never asked for.

Under this program I functioned as director of relief.

At this time Henry H. Blood was chairman of the State Road Commission. He had demonstrated his ability as an administrator to the point that he was recognized throughout the nation, becoming president of the American Association of Highway Officials. It was my opinion that he would make an outstanding governor, and I did everything I could to convince him to run, insisting, "Henry, I am not asking you to do anything I wouldn't do if you are elected and call on me."

At this time in history, however, it was in the state convention that party candidates were nominated, and Clarence Nelsen had tied up enough delegates to be nominated.

Blood agreed to stand for the nomination and, if we were successful in nominating him, to run for governor. Well, he was nominated and elected, and on January 2, 1933, he was inaugurated the seventh governor of the Beehive State.

I had barely returned to Ogden to my automobile business when I was surprised by a telephone call from Governor Blood from Washington, reminding me that I had agreed to do any thing I could for him should he be elected. The first thing he said he would like me to do was visit all the counties and get them organized to enroll men and boys in the Civil Conservation Corps (CCC).

The Civil Conservation Corps was an emergency conservation work organization created by President Roosevelt in April 1933 to relieve the acute conditions of widespread unemployment and to provide for the restoration of the country's depleted natural resources. Unemployed men between the ages of eighteen and twenty-five were enrolled in the organization for periods of six months. At the peak of the program, in January 1934, some 312,000 were enrolled in 1,466 camps—one third of which were in the far West.

Each worker received a cash allowance of $30 per month, of which at least $23 had to be allocated to his dependents. In addition he received food, clothing, shelter, and medical care, and in most camps he had an opportunity for education and research. In each camp was a library with reading material, books for study, and bulletins on forestry, parks, and other vocational subjects. Motion pictures illustrating practical forest and park activities were provided from time to time by the forestry and park agencies, and night classes were conducted in individual camps by the camp educational adviser, members of the park staffs, the army, and members of the CCC. In many camps there were also opportunities for attendance at lectures or classes in colleges and public schools in neighboring communities.

The men worked five days a week, eight hours a day, including travel time from camp to work and return.

The CCC gave men from all walks of life an opportunity for a fresh start in the outdoors. No experience was necessary for employment. The work was largely manual, and more than fifty different kinds of jobs were available, including construction of firebreaks, telephone systems, lookout stations, installation of minor dams and planting of trees and other vegetative cover to check erosion and diminish floods, general cleanup work, and construction of thousands of miles of trails.

In my own state, an extensive flood-control program was carried out over a large area of watershed lands in Davis County by CCC camp workers. Erosion-control work was done along the channel of the Virgin River in Orderville in Southern Utah, making the river water available for irrigation purposes. Two erosion dams were built in Salina Canyon, Sevier County, where other projects, including the installation of a telephone line from Mountain Ranch to the Gooseberry Range Station, were completed.

This public project turned out to be one of the finest things ever done. Not only did thousands of men receive employment for the first time in months, but long-overdue work was done in the forests and on public lands. It was a plus program all the way. However, only men could be employed in the CCC. In the meantime families were starving to death, and Roosevelt had promised, "No one will go hungry in America."

When I was organizing the counties for involvement in the CCC, Governor Blood asked me to take a look at the relief situation in each county because the Federal Government was going to pass a relief act soon. Sure enough, on May 12, 1933, just as I was getting ready to return to my business in Ogden, President Roosevelt—two months after his inauguration—approved the Federal Emergency Relief Act (FERA), which Congress had passed days earlier, and appropriated $500 million to help the states meet their immediate relief needs.

On May 22, 1933, Harry Hopkins, who had served as Roosevelt's director of relief in New York State, began administering federal relief. In his first two hours in office, he distributed $5 million. Before the end of his first year, he had disposed of $900 million and was demanding $950 million more. In the four years of the Relief Administration, Congress allocated more than $6 billion for the relief of more than four million destitute families who looked to the Federal Government for their very existence.

The funds were expended in two ways. First, money was given to the states on the basis of one dollar for every three dollars the states themselves appropriated and used for relief. Second, funds were used by Hopkins for direct grants to states when each state's governor proved his state no longer had financial means for necessary relief. Of the two methods, the second became the most important, and soon the funds were distributed by the Federal Relief Agency on a direct rather than matching basis. More than eighteen million persons received direct relief in this program.

Governor Blood asked me to set up the Utah Relief Organization on a business basis, so that there could be no unnecessary organizing, or boondoggling. I was willing to do this, but requested his help in securing a competent secretary—one familiar with state government. Jake Parker was given the assignment, and he obtained Mildred Showaker from the Utah State Road Commission. She was talented and capable and continued in the administration with Darrell Greenwell after I left. And as a matter of fact, Darrell told me on more than one occasion that he couldn't have taken over the responsibility of the state leadership without the help of Mildred. (On my return to Utah from government service and as an officer in ABC, I enlisted in Mildred's service again, and she has continued as my secretary.

When I had completed the assignment Blood gave me, I asked to be released so I could return to my own business. But I was informed that this was impossible because the Civil Works Administration (CWA) had been born, and the governor wanted me to stay on to administer its programs.

The Civil Works Administration, initiated to help the unemployed survive the critical winter of 1933-34, was quite different from the FERA in that the CWA was entirely federal, while FERA was a federal, state, and local cooperative program. Hopkins, not the governors, appointed state CWA administrators, and then state administrators helped select local personnel.

Hopkins hated the "hand-out," the dole. He believed that most Americans wanted to contribute to their nation's well-being, so the CWA became a work relief program, unlike FERA, which allocated funds on a direct relief basis. The CWA was set up to put money quickly into the hands of the millions who worked for it and would spend it on the basic needs of life. The government hoped it would be spent as quickly as possible, adding a boom to the economy until the winter was over and seasonal employment increased.

Nearly a billion dollars, provided from several sources, were allocated through CWA. The federal government provided 90 percent of the total. First the President transferred $400 million from the Public Works Administration. Hopkins made an additional $88,960,000 available by taking back unused FERA grants to states. And by a special act of February 15, 1934, Congress provided another $345 million. The states and local governments contributed the remaining 10 percent, nearly $90 million.

At least half the persons put to work on CWA were already on relief; the rest, unemployed but not on relief, were selected largely by the U.S. Employment Service. Local projects had to receive the approval of the state CWA officials, and then local wage rates, cost of materials, and types of projects affected the amount of funds a state received. More than 80 percent of the CWA expenditures went for completion of projects involving improvement on public property and development of recreational facilities. CWA nationally built and repaired 40,000 schools and 255,000 miles of roads and streets, built 469 airports and improved 529 others, laid 12 million feet of sewer pipe, and set up 3,500 playgrounds and athletic fields. More than 50,000 teachers were employed so that many rural schools could remain open. Some rural schools, such as those in Southern Utah, would have been forced to close if the funds had not been made available. Adults throughout the nation—2,000 in Salt Lake City alone—were taught new trades and skills as well as the usual literacy subjects when CWA funds were issued for free training.

The lift in morale caused by CWA projects was unmeasurable; it improved the lives of more than sixteen million Americans, and gave a tremendous psychological boost to men who had the chance to work for money rather than stand in line for it. Some people said this made the program worth its cost. Others, however, criticized it severely. They argued that many more people wanted to work on CWA projects than could be employed. Others said CWA caused localities to dump their relief problems on the federal government, thus discouraging private building. There was criticism because eleven states received 57 percent of the total spent by CWA and because 39 percent of the total went to ninety-three large cities with the highest density of unemployment. Some insisted CWA wages were too high—that thousands of men working for CWA were receiving more money per week than they had ever received in their lives, and so they passed up opportunities for private employment. CWA projects were not under contract. Because officials had little time to check projects sponsored by local and state agencies, leaf raking occurred—something else the public complained about.

In California, June 20, 1934, R.C. Branion, state emergency relief director, and eight other high officials of the CWA were indicted by the Federal Grand Jury on charges of conspiracy to defraud the government.

The Salt Lake *Telegram,* June 21, 1934, reported, "The first indictment charged that defendants permitted the expenditure of CWA funds for the employment of men on projects not approved, sent them to work without plans or tools, forcing them to remain idle, while paying them $500,000 for labor not performed and causing their activities to be reported falsely by timekeepers.

"The second indictment alleged that employment offices were established without authority, CWA work orders were issued to improperly registered persons, that FERA officials tampered with ratings, caused work orders to be issued in excess of the allotment of 60,000 and issued 32,000 illegal orders."

Hopkins probably never succeeded in getting all people to appreciate the good of CWA; and because it was expensive, Roosevelt discontinued it as an economic measure as soon as it had served its purpose. However, Hopkins was able to continue CWA under the FERA in a modified form, as experience had shown that many people in need came to relief stations only if work was available.

So, in the spring of 1934, many projects not completed by the CWA were continued and expanded under FERA sponsorship. Most FERA projects, however, were new.

Work on public property provided the bulk of employment for the "new" FERA, with construction projects of recreational facilities, conservation projects, federal buildings, highways, and airports emphasized. However, one percent of the projects were for skilled or professionally trained unemployed, including architects, engineers, and the like. Production-for-use activities were also introduced, and more than 1,000,000 articles of infant wear, 3,500,000 women's and girls' dresses, 1,000,000 men's and boys' shirts, 1,250,000 mattresses, 5,000,000 pillow cases, and 4,000,000 sheets were made. The FERA distributed these goods to families on relief.

In the mattress-production project, the federal government made contracts with the factories, who did the picking and blowing of the cotton into the ticks, the end sewing, and the beating and tufting. The contractor was paid about $2.27 for each mattress for these operations. The relief workers cut and sewed the ticks in the factory workrooms and did the roll-edging, side stitching, and labeling.

In Utah, the Salt Lake Mattress Company, Cramer Bedding Company, Stover Bedding Company, Intermountain Mattress Company, and New Life Bedding Company were involved in the project, and in Salt Lake City alone by November 19, 1934, more than 2,036 mattresses were produced.

Both the white-collar projects and production-for-use activities received considerable criticism, especially from persons who maintained that work relief costs more than direct cash relief. Hopkins's reply to the widespread criticism was, "The FERA had to provide mattresses and related items in this way or not at all. The only alternative was to increase the amount FERA could spend for relief."

Hopkins believed there were differences in human capabilities and interests and that the best relief program would recognize these differences, allowing people to use the tools they knew well. This way they could more quickly work their way back to a better life. He understood that if violinists and sculptors were put to work with picks and shovels, not only would they dig poor ditches, but their skilled fingers would also become hardened and stiff, permanently unfit to resume their real life work.

When the work of FERA came to a halt in the summer of 1935, nearly 240,000 projects had been completed, representing an expenditure of $1.3 billion. Two million men and women had been employed, and farmers suffering losses from droughts had been aided.

Works Work Relief vs "Dole"

Wanted: Not a red cent of federal dole for Mormon Utah, Idaho, Arizona or California.
    —Heber J. Grant (New York *Daily News,* 6-20-38)

In the spring of 1934, Utah was hit with a serious drought, caused by a light snowfall during the winter before. We had never had anything like it. As rainless weeks and record-breaking temperatures dragged on and on, orchards withered, permanent crops burned up, and it became impossible to do anything except use to best possible advantage whatever had been left. Ranchers were forced to abandon their ranches for lack of culinary or stock water. In Davis County alone there were 200 families taking culinary water from irrigation ditches. Livestock on farms and small dairies, and range cattle died; their owners ran out of funds. It got to the point that rain would improve crops and ranges, but could not mature the crops. The situation was that critical.

To find a solution, the good citizens knowledgeable on water matters assembled and established the Water Conservation and Development Program, which we felt—had we the money to bring it about—would solve the drought problems and save the federal government from having to increase our regular relief allotments to meet the additional burden of feeding drought victims in distress. Helping me to develop and put the program in motion were William Peterson, director of extension at the Agriculture College in

Logan; Tom H. Humphrey, state engineer, and members of his staff; William R. Wallace, chairman, Utah Water Storage Commission; and Herbert Barns and Frank H. Jugler, canners.

I was unacquainted with Harry Hopkins at the time, but called him on the telephone and told him if he would give us $600,000, we would save him $3 million in direct relief. Hopkins said if the program looked as good on paper as it sounded over the phone, we had the money. And eventually we did have the money. We went through with the program and did even better than I had told Hopkins we would.

The Water Development and Conservation Program did exactly what its name implied—conserved every drop of water in the state. We did this by tightening up in all areas, repairing all leaks in canals and irrigation ditches, cleaning springs, draining marshes, and cutting production. The more important projects included opening a new channel from Strawberry Reservoir to the tunnel portal and draining Provo Bay to augment the supply of Utah Lake. We also launched a cattle purchasing and slaughtering program, and all livestock that otherwise would have perished from lack of feed were slaughtered and canned. Although it was not prime beef, not even choice, it was good, wholesome, and palatable and was given to people on relief. Thus, the program served two good purposes; it conserved cattle, and it fed the hungry.

As a result of the program's success, Hopkins called me one day and asked me to go out and do in the other drought-stricken states what we had done in Utah. I told him it wouldn't be easy as we had more talent to develop and conserve water in Utah than in the other states. Besides, I wanted to go home to my business and family in Ogden. He just laughed and said, "I understand you are a man who likes to ride planes. You can go home every weekend."

There was no talking him out of it. To make a long story short, I wound up as administrator of seven Western states—Idaho, Utah, Arizona, New Mexico, Colorado, Wyoming, and Montana. It wasn't long before I was made regional administrator of the eleven western states and of Hawaii and Alaska and, as such, Hopkins's assistant administrator of FERA. This was Hopkins's plan to get me to Washington on a permanent basis.

So I relinquished my position as state administrator and took a suite first in the Hay Adams Hotel, and then in the Mayflower Hotel in Washington, D.C., and borrowed Darrell Greenwell from the Ogden *Standard Examiner* for a year to run relief programs in Utah. Darrell was a person with great talent and unusual integrity, and he remained state director practically as long as the federal government was involved in relief.

We never sold our house in Ogden. Clarissa, with her superb managerial ability, took over the dealership, stepping into business at a time when few women did. She made it

The Hinckley family with Harry Hopkins

51

a success, gaining more admiration than criticism. She also kept complete control of her children, even though she never discouraged their monkeyshine and never discouraged them from heckling each other. Even though Betty would sometimes call for help, her mother would leave it up to her to settle her differences with her three brothers. She did—and usually came out the victor. I was much more stern in disciplining, but only spanked one child, Paul, after he provoked me to my limit. It was a great mistake, however, and truly made me ill.

Clarissa had a tremendous sense of the right values and was very practical, able to see through to the core of problems and simplify them. Her philosophy was a happy family, and because they were brought up in such a comfortable way, our children never caused us any trouble or grief.

Although I had to be away from home a great deal of time, we kept very close as a family. Clarissa spent as much time with me in the East as she could, often leaving Ogden at the drop of a hat when I needed or wanted her with me. On one occasion, when she had to pack and leave within a matter of minutes, she left a note on the kitchen table for Betty. It read, "I have gone to wash. [no capital] I will see you soon." In another family this might have meant that the mother had gone to do the laundry. To Betty it meant her mother had gone east and that Betty was in charge until Clarissa returned.

There was no show or sham about Clarissa when she came to Washington; she was the same person no matter who she was with. That's the reason everyone loved her. Clarissa would go to Washington and still be the country girl she was. Yet she loved pretty things, especially hats. But she loved her friends, too, so if a lady friend truly admired her hat, she'd take it off and give it to her. This always created laughs and fun and happiness. That was Clarissa—warm and fun-loving.

On special occasions, such as presidential inaugurations, the children would accompany her to the nation's capital. At Roosevelt's fourth-term inauguration, the family watched Robert march in the parade as a cadet from West Point. It was an exciting time for my children.

Often when I was in the FERA, and later in the Works Progress Administration (WPA), we would plan trips around my schedule. When I visited the northwest states, Clarissa and the children would take up residency some place on the beach near Portland. If I had to be on the West Coast, she would start the family tour in San Francisco and wind up in San Diego. I would be with them most of the way, working out of their vacation spot.

I must have stressed education, because all four children are well educated. Robert had a year at Stanford before he got his appointment to West Point, where he graduated. When he returned from the war, the Air Corps thought he was good enough for them to send him to the University of Chicago School of Business, where he received degrees in production management and personnel management, graduating in the top ten of his class. Betty graduated cum laude from the University of Utah, where in her senior year she was vice-president of the student body. John and Paul attended the New Mexico Military Institute. Then John went to Ft. Benning, Georgia, where he received his officer's commission as a lieutenant in the Army. After the war he graduated from the University of Utah. Paul graduated from West Point and was commissioned in the U.S. Air Force.

All four children were better educated than I.

As assistant administrator of FERA and subsequently the WPA, I developed a warm, friendly relationship with Hopkins, and always when I was in Washington, I would spend at least one evening with Harry and his wife, Barbara, who lived in the Kennedy Warren Apartments. (Barbara Duncan was the second wife of the WPA head; they had married in 1931). What a beautiful couple they were. But although Harry had indomitable energy, he was lean and frail and abused himself with long working hours and irregular eating habits. His diet consisted mostly of small amounts of food, coffee, cigarettes and paregoric, so Mrs. Hopkins always concerned herself about his health. She had a great trick. In the evenings, when I had finished dining with them, she would leave to walk the dog and I would accompany her for a while so she could ask me about Harry's health—how he was performing and all. The ironic thing about this is that Mrs. Hopkins preceded Harry in death. She died October 7, 1937, with her husband at her bedside.

Hopkins was one of the great men in government in that era. Although he was maligned and downgraded—some of it being his own fault because he didn't care what others thought and he gave little thought to the niceties of diplomacy—he was a doer, and that's the reason Roosevelt liked him. He not only did his own job; he was alert to everything else the President expected done and would see that it got done. If the persons responsible for that job didn't like Hopkins's intrusion, they might argue later, but in the meantime Hopkins would see that the job was done. He wanted results, and he wanted them *now*. He would grasp a situation and would respond immediately by getting a project unerway—unlike Roosevelt, who would sometimes procrastinate—even though at times that was a good thing. And like Roosevelt, Hopkins believed that man-to-man diplomacy worked.

Had it not been for Hopkins, it's difficult to believe that Roosevelt could have come up with the relief programs he did. Roosevelt and Hopkins together are the reason America didn't go communistic. During the Hoover Administration, the American populace was ready to go communistic. "Why not?" people were asking. It could be no worse than starving to death. It was Hopkins who kept Roosevelt's ear attuned to the one-third of the nation who were ill-housed, ill-fed, and ill-clothed.

In addition to Hopkins, President Roosevelt surrounded himself with other doers, two of whom were Thomas G. Corcoran and his associate Benjamin V. Cohen. Corcoran, whom Roosevelt christened "Tommy the Cork,"[6] was a bright young Harvard Law School graduate who became a free-wheeling New Dealer, known to many as the President's special guy. The undoubted triumph of his public career was joint authorship with Cohen of the Utility Holding Company Act of 1935—the biggest bill ever enacted into law up to 1941. It was sixty-five pages long and its language so technical nobody in Congress even pretended to debate its terms in detail. There was no doubt Corcoran was a doer. On August 10, 1941, the New York *Times Herald* reported, "Tommy Corcoran was a man sought after as no other less than the President himself. He was a Keeper of Official Secrets, a Molder of Public Powers.

"Corcoran and Cohen were making law by order of the President and then having it ratified by Congress."

Corcoran wouldn't stop doing something just because someone said, "You can't do that; it's not legal." He would make it legal if possible to get the job done. He used to say, "If it's legal, give it to Ben. If it's not legal, give it to me." Both men were talented lawyers, and even their worst enemies wouldn't deny their charm.

During the time I was associated with Hopkins, he was in and out of the White House, living there for a period after the death of Barbara. And on many occasions when there was nothing else doing, he would take me there for dinner with the President and Mrs. Roosevelt. The President was good-natured most of the time, often flashing that cheery smile and hearty laugh—the confidence and optimism that were a comfort to the American people. Although his legs were immobilized by polio in 1921, he never sulked or complained and didn't show his ailments until the end. In fact, often the President's face was a mask, not revealing any emotion on a specific subject. At other times, however, I could see his anguish or anger, for his heavy Dutch chin

---

6. Roosevelt had a hobby of nicknaming those close to him. Hopkins was "Harry to Hop"; Harold Ickes was "Harry the Ick."

would double up.

The conversation at dinner was lively—not only about what was going on in the country, but what more the country needed and what could be done to meet those needs. Mrs. Roosevelt said her husband wanted to be remembered as having served the actual betterment of mankind; that was his deepest motivation. It was also Mrs. Roosevelt's goal, so the conversation was always interesting. The aggressive first lady had become a full partner in the Roosevelt Team. She had joined the Womans Trade Union League and the State Democratic Committee. She was an expert on hospitals, prisons, and schools, and she favored more rights for women and people who were poor or in trouble. Although her family inheritance was almost wiped out by the 1929 market crash, she used her personal income to give work and help to individuals who could not be helped through regular channels.

Together Hopkins and Roosevelt were an unbeatable pair. Whenever I felt that I had served in government long enough—when I would try to get back home—Hopkins would take me over to the White House (he'd have the President set up in advance), and he and Roosevelt would talk me out of it. They were a combination I couldn't compete with.

While the FERA had shown the value of work relief vs direct relief, Hopkins felt that new work programs and methods were necessary. So on May 6, 1935, the Works Progress Administration (WPA) was established to operate a nationwide program of small useful projects designed to provide employment for the 3,500,000 unemployed. WPA lived in the future. The administration seldom consulted past records of relief programs, did most of the business by phone, and kept no records of it.

The major operating unit was the state, which served as the centralized agency between the local, district offices and Washington. Below the state level the main organization was the district. Projects had to be useful and had to

President Franklin D. Roosevelt

require a large proportion of funds for wages and a low proportion for materials. The projects most preferred were those in which in which the local sponsor contributed a fair share of the cost and those which would give a financial return to the federal treasury. WPA sponsored a larger conglomeration of projects than any other single government agency had done before in American history. The projects ranged from building bridges to draining huge swamp areas (advancing the fight against malaria by thirty years) to painting murals in public buildings; from performing symphonies to teaching adults to read and write, to building airports.

Region Five, the Western States, of which I was in charge, led the whole country in projects of lasting value, including airports, which in that day were not in immediate need, but which soon became overcrowded. Airports, built in practically every city of any size in the Western States, were the best work projects we had in WPA, and they never stopped paying dividends on the relief funds spent constructing them. As indicated on a plaque on the east side of the Salt Lake Airport, it is one of these. So was the Ogden Airport—which was named Hinckley Field April 10, 1942, and remained such until Harmon Perry became mayor of Ogden.

In the East, WPA work projects were difficult to establish because of the dense population, and leaf raking occurred. This, however, was not true of Region Five, which included only 10 percent of the nation's population and 40 percent of the area. Lasting projects, such as highways, reservoirs, and other water-conservation projects were easy to develop and had immediate use and lasting nature that would pay dividends on the expenditures forever.

WPA projects were for both men and women, but some 90-95 percent of the workers came from relief rolls, and because most of the workers were semiskilled and unskilled, projects had to be limited in scope. However, Hopkins also initiated Federal Arts Projects to provide employment for the 30,000 unemployed musicians, painters, actors, and writers—one or two percent of the population.

The artists' condition was this: for decades the nation's recognition and appreciation of them had grown steadily. Then suddenly, with the market crash, the subsidies, the golden horseshoes, and the box-parties were gone—gone just at the time when America's inventive genius was reproducing plays on celluloid and shipping them everywhere in tin cans, or sending the music of a single orchestra to the far corners of the earth on waves of the air. The painters and sculptors lost their patrons, and when the volume of advertising shrank to a mere shadow of its former self, newspapers and magazines needed only a fraction of the articles and stories they had bought from American writers during the gay twenties.

So in launching WPA, Hopkins had enough courage to stand in the face of constant criticism and say, "White-collar people get hungry, too, and they shall be fed along with all the others." This was in line with Roosevelt's policy that no one would go hungry in America.

No one knew what the result of the Federal Arts Project would be, but once the orchestras began to play, many people began listening to them. Writers began visiting out-of-the-way places, asking questions, listening to stories to write the American Guide (a tour guide). In Utah, the Utah State Institute of Fine Arts was the statewide sponsor of the Utah Writers Project. The guide, which highlighted the state's places, resources, and people, was one of a series prepared especially for automobile travelers on hard roads in the forty-eight states. It warned the traveler of rough stretches, quicksands and waterless deserts.

The book had indeed a collective author. Local, county, state, and federal agencies, transportation agencies, and hundreds of individuals were of assistance in furnishing and checking material.

The Utah Art Project prepared the art work and maps in the book; the Utah Historical Record Survey opened its files for much historical data and helped the writers project prepare the history essay, the chronology, and the selected reading list. The Utah Adult Education Project provided the services of one of their employees for writing the articles on geography and climate, and a member of the WPA Division of Operations prepared the article on irrigation. The writers, however, were not permitted to be identified with their works.

The first state director of the Writers Project was Maurice L. Howe (1935-38), and he was followed by Charles K. Madsen (1940), Dale Morgan (1942), and Mrs. Grace Winkleman Byrne (1943).

Through the Federal Arts Project, teachers of music whose pupils could no longer pay for lessons began organizing community sings and choral groups. Along the blank walls of many a public building, after the plastering was done, mural painters set up their scaffoldings and mixed their paints, and millions in the country who had never seen an original oil painting were able to.

There were student projects and women's projects. The construction of the sand fill and the seawall on the Shoals northwest of Yerba Buena Island to prepare a permanent airport and recreational facility for the city and county of San Francisco was also a WPA project.

Because the immediate purpose for Treasure Island (as Yerba Buena was called) was to be the site of the 1940 Golden Gate International Exposition, I met with the head of the exposition, Leland Cutler, on his various trips to Washington, to do all possible to get funds to prepare the island as the site. Cutler was a friend of President Hoover and a former chairman and member of the board of trustees of Stanford University, and during our meetings we developed a close relationship.

The commissioner of the exposition was George Creel, another dear friend, who was a great supporter of California Senator William Gibbs McAdoo, Woodrow Wilson's son-in-law. Once when Creel came to Washington, the two of us visited the senator, who suggested we drop in on Vice-President James Garner, who was presiding in the Senate. Garner left the floor and received us in his office, where he got out a demijohn filled with what I assume was bootleg whiskey. (Of course, it may be that it was the very best and that that was just his method of storing and handling it.) Garner put out four tumblers. We were permitted to pour our own, fortunately, and then, to quote the vice-president, "We together struck a blow for liberty!"

As administrator of the eleven western states, I thought it advisable to employ an army engineer, if possible, to assist with the projects. Hopkins said it couldn't be done, but with the help of Colonel Lawrence Westbrook, a member of Hopkins's staff, I was successful in obtaining Lieutenant Colonel Donald M. Connolly, who was useful in organizing the state engineering department in the eleven states. Before this was completed, however, trouble broke out in California.

In Los Angeles many minority groups were crying out for things they were not entitled to, but they were making such a clamor that it was easy for the administration in Washington to think all hell had broken loose in Los Angeles. As a result, I decided to divide the state into northern and southern California, leaving Frank Y. McLaughlin as administrator of relief in Northern California with headquarters in San Francisco, and putting Connolly in charge of Southern California with headquarters in Los Angeles. To begin with there was a great uproar, stirred up by the minority groups, over our bringing in an outsider—and an army officer at that!—to administer California relief. However, in no time at all everything was going smoothly because Connolly organized his administration properly and listened to all groups, and because the residents soon discovered that he was not only competent, but honest and dependable. I had intended to leave the colonel there only until we could find someone to succeed him, but he stayed for many years. When he departed, newspapers and the minority groups complained just as bitterly and loudly that he was going to be taken away, as they had when he was initially installed.

As a result of the foregoing success, I was surprised to get a call from Hopkins, who said, "Can you be in my office tomorrow at 11:00 a.m.?" I said that if I could get transportation (I was somewhere in the West), I'd be there. I got there, arriving a few minutes ahead of the appointed time. Hopkins told me that the purpose of the meeting was to convince General Edward W. Markham, chief of the Corps of Engineers, to permit his men to come into WPA, which we both felt was only natural, because WPA had more money than the Engineers had up to that time, and the Engineers were skilled in doing civilian work.

The general arrived with his aide, Captain Lucius Clay, and after an hour's meeting, the Engineers were in WPA, and I returned to the eleven western states with seventeen army engineers instead of one. Every state was assigned one or two engineers, who saw that the projects were properly supervised, planned, and followed through until completion. If I had any claim to fame in WPA work, this is it.

Periodically after the Engineers came into WPA, General Markham would make a demand on Hopkins for their return to army work. Each time, Hopkins would call on me to meet with the general and pacify him. The last such meeting was in San Francisco. I made an appointment with the general at the St. Frances Hotel, and during a congenial breakfast, I told him a story that had recently happened in Washington. Nels Anderson, one of Hopkins's labor representatives, was in a meeting I attended one day, and was reaching for an expletive to describe someone he had absolutely no respect for. "I'll tell you what kind of a son-of-a-bitch he is," Anderson said. "He's the kind of a son-of-a-bitch I thought the army was before I met the Army Engineers."

This story apparently made the sale, for we had no more difficulty keeping the Army Engineers supervising WPA work. Markham himself told this story wherever he went, and I heard it time and time again.

Like Los Angeles, San Francisco also suffered troublesome times during my term as assistant administrator of WPA. In the mid-1930s there was a general strike. Milk trucks were being turned over at the edge of the city and nothing was being permitted to come in at all in the way of food products. President Roosevelt was in Hawaii; Hopkins was in Europe. I represented the federal government at the scene, and I practically lived in City Hall (the Taylor Hotel, where I was staying, was across the street) with San Francisco Mayor Angelo J. Rossi (Bald and a bit portly, he was a delightful man who became a loveable friend.) He was on top of the situation and had his people doing all possible on all fronts. To help him ease tension, I made a statement from the steps of City Hall that no one would go hungry in San Francisco.

During the strike I was called by Aubrey Williams, second man in WPA, who said they were just going into a cabinet meeting to see whether or not to ask the President to come back to settle the strike. I said, "Hell's bells, Aubrey. It will soon be that you can't go out to pee without a presidential decree." After rollicking laughter, Aubrey said, "I wish I could use that in the cabinet meeting, but Frances Perkins will be there." (Mrs. Perkins was Secretary of Labor).

After the strike was settled, California Senator Hyrum Johnson said, "I was intrigued with your statement that no one will go hungry in San Francisco. How were you going to see to this?" I replied that I was simply extending to the city level the Roosevelt Doctrine that no one will go hungry in America. But in the back of my mind I kept remembering that Secretary of War George Dern was my friend.

When Roosevelt returned from Hawaii, I joined him in Seattle, where we began a trip across the country, visiting all the WPA projects. One of our stops was in Rochester, Minnesota, where the President participated in the dedication of the carillon bells on the Mayo Clinic. It was then that I first met Dr. Charles Mayo. I later returned to the clinic for a physical checkup and was told I had a goiter.

San Francisco Mayor Angelo J. Rossi

Dr. Mayo was called in for consultation, and he recommended I have it removed, as one in sixteen are malignant. Upon returning to Washington, I told Hopkins the situation, but he advised against the operation, insisting I could lose my voice permanently. He then sent me to the Lahey Clinic in Boston, where Dr. Frank Howard Lahey gave me the same diagnosis I had received at Mayo.

It was not until a year after I had returned to Mayo and had the operation, that I told Dr. Mayo all the details of the incident. He never quite got over it, and constantly ribbed me about not having enough confidence in the Mayo Clinic to go ahead on his advice. It was on account of the early acquaintance that we became good friends and I had an annual checkup. Thanks to those yearly examinations I am alive today.

The Roosevelt Administration gave more time, effort, and money to WPA than to any other of the relief and work relief agencies, and it received the most criticism as it was the most extensive. Many said WPA became a haven of refuge for persons who never made a really serious attempt to find private employment. A great number of WPA workers did refuse private jobs because WPA wages were higher, but Hopkins made a ruling that if a worker refused suitable private employment, he would be dismissed from WPA.

The WPA was accused of being a communist organization, and of course Hopkins and Roosevelt were both accused of being communists or, if not communists, socialists. The principal criticism came after there had been many successes in the relief program: prior to that time people were so desolate that they questioned nothing, but after they were convinced that the administration wouldn't let them go hungry, they became quite outspoken.

In my own state, the president of the Mormon Church led the criticism. Not since the old polygamy days had the church made headlines as frequently as it did during the WPA era. Heber J. Grant, who became president of the church on November 23, 1918, undertook the task of selling the more than 500,000 Mormons in Utah, Idaho, Arizona, and California the idea of lifting themselves by their own bootstraps rather than accepting government largesse. His contention was that the dole, as he called it, was "sapping national morale," and he sought to reinvoke the sturdy individualism of the pioneer days, the spirit that pushed the American frontier across the plains and prairies, through the wilderness and desert, and over the Rockies and Sierras to the Pacific Coast. Quoting the first two lines of a famous Mormon hymn, "Come, Come Ye Saints, No Toil Nor Labor Fear," Grant would say, "May that sink deep, may that sink very deep into the hearts of all Latter-day Saints who are now on doles."

However, although it ridiculed federal work projects, the church attempted to solve the unemployment problem among Mormons by creating projects of its own through a social security program. Projects ranged from coal mining and sugar-beet raising to the manufacturing of temple clothing. But the program was entirely cooperative, without any cash remuneration. The unemployed members worked on church projects and received for their labor foodstuffs, clothing, and other commodities donated by the more fortunate brethren and stored in surplus warehouses.

Despite the program, however, there were church members working in WPA. David O. McKay, a counselor to President Grant, and one of the three known officially as the First Presidency, representing the top hierarchy of the church, told of a couple of these men in an article published by the New York *Daily News* on June 20, 1938. McKay said, "I own a farm at Huntsville, northeast of Ogden (Utah). I was up there the other day and my neighbor told me he was trying to get a ditch dug but couldn't get anyone to do the job.

"What's the matter with so-and-so?," I asked him. "He hasn't been working."

"Oh, I went after him," said my neighbor, "but he turned me down. He's on WPA now. He's pulling weeds five days a week."

"Well," I said, "how about his son? He's been doing nothing."

"Yes, I know," my neighbor replied. "But he got on WPA too. They're both pulling weeds."

"So," continued McKay, "I jumped in and helped dig the ditch. I think that incident is typical of the situation in Utah and elsewhere. We're building a population of loafers, a professional dole class. Once they get on WPA, they don't want to get off."

The paper continued by stating that McKay's conclusions paralleled those of Grant, who was fond of recounting how he watched a WPA crew at work excavating and had counted up to as high as forty between shovelfuls.

In the same article in the *Daily News,* Darrell J. Greenwell, state WPA administrator, took sharp issue with the church officials, citing the records of his office. He said, "In November of 1935, the peak of WPA employment for Utah, the rolls showed a total of 16,400 persons. By November 1937 the number had diminished to 6,000.

"There," said Greenwell, "is the answer to the charge that these people won't take private employment, because more than 10,000 of them did. And 75 percent of them were Mormons. Today in Utah, we have approximately 11,000 on WPA and the percentage of Mormons remains the same. Church officials will tell you these people are in bad standing. Nevertheless, the church counts them in when giving out its membership figures."

A postcard census conducted by John D. Biggers in 1938 showed that Utah, with a population of close to 525,000, was nearly 65 percent Mormon. The census showed that in the state there were 18,916 persons totally unemployed and 11,003 emergency workers, meaning enrollees of the WPA, CCC and NYA (National Youth Administration) and 13,607 partly employed. Biggers's census revealed Utah as one of the eight states with the highest percentage of population on federal emergency work rolls. WPA was spending about $600,000 a month there during this period.

When I first accepted the responsibility of the eleven western states and the territories of Alaska and Hawaii, in addition to my responsibilities as assistant administrator of FERA and WPA, Hopkins told me I could establish an office where it was most convenient to cover the area. That, in my opinion, was Salt Lake City. As a result, the office was moved from San Francisco to Salt Lake City, where it remained until I was put out of circulation by an automobile accident. I was returning one night from Salt Lake City to Ogden. A dairy farmer, who had waited for a passing train, whisked his cattle across the highway without any regard for traffic. There was a curve in the road, also a change in the grade uphill. Consequently, my automobile headlights didn't reflect on the road, but directly above it. The dairy herd was upon me before I could stop. Eight of my ribs were fractured in fourteen places in the collision, and while I was recuperating, I wound up with pleurisy.

Hopkins suggested I go to Hawaii and get some rest and inspect the relief situation there. In my absence Clinton Anderson, administrator of relief in New Mexico and my assistant, was to assume my responsibilities on the mainland. But in my absence (and in the absence of Hopkins), Aubrey Williams took it upon himself to change our plans. He discharged Anderson and put in his place a character by the name of R.C. Jacobson, who moved the regional office back to San Francisco.

I heard about it, returned home, and in June 1936 resigned.

Immediately Hopkins called me from Washington and did all possible to get me to reconsider; President Roosevelt wrote me a letter also importuning me to return. With these kinds of pressures, I returned to Hopkins's administration a few weeks later. Jacobson was relieved as a member of my staff; Anderson was brought back, and the office was resituated in Salt Lake City. Anderson later went on to become a congressman from New Mexico, secretary of agriculture under President Harry S. Truman, and a senator from New Mexico. That should indicate something about my judgment of the man, who obviously was a great citizen and great government servant.

The work relief projects of the WPA were wound up in December 1938. I, however, did not see them to the end.

Civil Aeronautics

One fact which stands out is that hardly another civil activity of our people bears such a direct and intimate relation to the national security as does civil aviation.
—Franklin D. Roosevelt (1939)

One spring day when I was home in Ogden having breakfast with Clarissa after the children had gone to school, Hopkins called to tell me that President Roosevelt was sending my name to the Senate as a member of the Civil Aeronautics Authority.

I immediately remonstrated, telling him if I were going to stay in government, which I was trying not to do, I would stay in an area I knew something about. The Civil Aeronautics Authority (CAA), created by the Civil Aeronautics Act of 1938, was another new agency—the first in our history established to regulate civil aviation.

All I could get out of Hopkins was, "Have you had your breakfast yet?" He wasn't about to be turned down.

"I was having my breakfast until I was so rudely interrupted," I replied. That terminated the conversation. Later, after talking it over with Clarissa, I called Hopkins back and told him to tell the President to take my name off the list—that getting into a new agency was no way to come home.

"Well, I'm sorry, Bob, but the names have already gone up," Hopkins said. Whether they had or not, I don't know, but that was his reply. Consequently, thirty-five years after

Orville and Wilbur Wright made their first flight in a heavier-than-air motor-driven plane at Kitty Hawk, North Carolina, I was named a member of the CAA and on August 8, 1938, was administered the oath of office by a Utahn, Associate Justice Harold H. Stephens of the U.S. Court of Appeals.

Named to chair the authority was Edward J. Noble, a liberal Republican and widely known industrialist and aviation enthusiast of New York State. Harlee Branch, second assistant postmaster general in charge of the department's airmail activities, was named vice-chairman. Other members of the group were G. Grant Mason of Washington, D.C., in charge of Pan American Airways Latin American Division, and Oswald Ryan of Anderson, Indiana, general counsel of the federal power commission. Clinton M. Hester was appointed administrator of the authority. Mr. Hester, assistant general counsel of the treasury from Montana, had no prior contact with aviation matters other than his experience during the ten months he helped draft the Lea Bill, from which the Civil Aeronautics Act was

Hinckley family during war years

largely derived.

We were appointed for a six-year term at $12,000 annually. At least this was the salary stipulated in the act. Later, however, Congress realized that this was $2,000 more than they were getting, so their appropriation limited our salaries to $10,000 a year.

The first actual contact I had with an airplane was some twenty-eight years before my appointment to the aviation authority. I attended the first International Air Meet held in the U.S. at Belmont Park, New York, when I was on my way to Germany as a Mormon missionary. Three years later at Templehof Feld in Berlin, I made my first flight, with Melli Beese, wife of the French airman Charles Boutard, and champion woman flyer of the world. My enthusiasm for flying led to the development of Utah-Pacific Airways with my friend Dean Brimhall before the depression, but despite this, there were those who didn't feel my credentials were sufficient.

Upon my appointment to the CAA, I, like the other new members, was criticized as lacking experience in the aviation industry. On July 27, 1938, the New York *Times* reported, "Individually all of these men are undoubtedly of high caliber and anxious to do a good job. As a commission to control aviation, however, the group is sadly out of balance. It would have been a great mistake to appoint a commission of all aviation people, but for the sake of the future of a business so tied up with our national economics and our national defense, there should be more aviation talent than turned up."

My appointment came as a complete surprise to Utah Senator William H. King, my mother's cousin (a senator for twenty-four years—the only one who ever introduced a bill to abolish the WPA) because my name had never been mentioned in connection with the authority. President Roosevelt had not consulted King, which was customary, and therefore didn't know King had both a Republican and Democratic candidate waiting in the wings. The Utah delegation had united in recommending the appointment of Darrel T. Lane of Salt Lake City, late of the Mexican Claims Commission. Lane, in addition to delegation support, had the backing of the assistant secretaries of war and commerce, the American Legion, and countless others.

But President Roosevelt couldn't have cared less. I was appointed to the authority, and Senator King never quite got over it.

The Civil Aeronautics Act of 1938 established the Civil Aeronautics Authority as an independent agency to promote the development, safety, and regulation of civil aeronautics and extended to the new agency a wide jurisdiction over the interstate, overseas, and international airlines of the U.S. For these carriers the agency was empowered to issue certificates of public convenience and necessity, fix rates for the carriage of air mail, and review or establish tariffs for other types of traffic.

The agency was also to regulate the corporate relationships between air carriers and other persons and to pass on loans to air carriers from the federal government. It was directed to frame and enforce regulations relating to the safety of all phases of air transportation operation, and likewise to take over the establishment, maintenance, and operation of all aids to air navigation along the Federal Airways System.

The agency was to issue certificates of airworthiness for civil aircraft and to examine and issue certificates of competency to civilian pilots. It was also given control over nonscheduled interstate commercial aviation. Its powers to frame safety regulations extended to all types of civilian flying and it was given the fullest powers to investigate aircraft accidents for the purpose of framing and enforcing such regulations. It was given a large degree of control over pilot and mechanic training agencies and was charged with the technical review and approval of all airport projects undertaken by federal work relief agencies.

The Washington National Airport came under this category. For years I had been needling Hopkins to construct an airport in Washington as I had done in the western states, because there was no place that needed an airport as badly as the nation's capital. Apparently the reason I was appointed to the authority was to build this airport, because as soon as I took office, Hopkins said, "Hinckley, if you're so smart, let's see you build an airport in Washington."

I said, "Do you mean it?"

"Sure, I do," he said, "and I will do all I can to help you."

We had just begun digging the first shovel of mud from Gravelly Point on the Potomac in November 1938, for construction of the Washington National Airport, when I received a call from Senator King.

"Son [he always called me son], what do you think you're doing?"

I asked what he meant.

"Well," he said, "you come to town, and overnight you start building an airport I have been studying for sixteen years. You don't know what you're doing, but you're going ahead anyway. I should have you investigated."

I said, "Please, senator, wait until the airport is completed and then let's go on with the investigation. I'll have plenty of time after that."

We were always friends after a fashion. King was always a pompous guy, and I was always "son." I never grew up; I remained Addie's boy.

At this time, Hopkins was Secretary of Commerce (he was appointed in 1938 and resigned in 1940), and Colonel F. C. Harrington was administrator of the Works Progress Administration. We laid out a plan to build the airport with Harrington giving us as much WPA money as possible, the President giving us as much money from the Public Works Program as possible, and the Army Engineers were doing the actual work. The construction of the airport involved a type of work that the Corps of Engineers had long experience in, as it was similar to operations accomplished for many years by the Corps in its river and harbor and flood-control work.

The airport was completed in 1940—only to be denounced by many. Nevertheless, on September 9 of that year, about 15,000 spectators saw 400 Army and Navy planes criss-cross in the air. I rode in one of seven big air transports that also carried Donald M. Connolly, Edward Noble, Clinton M. Hester, and other guests over the field. When President Roosevelt ordered the transports to land, the field was officially opened. Then, emphasizing preparedness, the President said, "A proper and adequate flying field has been a Washington problem since the Wrights had their first crash on the parade ground at Fort Myer thirty years ago. Two years ago, the problem became so acute as literally to give me bad dreams. So, upon the passage of the Civil Aeronautics Act, one of the first tasks I asked of the new agency was the creation of an adequate airport for the nation's capital. That was in August. On November 19, 1938, I watched a dredge bring the first mucky soil from beneath some ten feet of water very near the spot where we now stand. They told me this field would be usable within two years. Today, well within that promise, the field was used. It will be in regular use within three more months. And Assistant Secretary Hinckley [I was made assistant secretary of commerce for air in 1940 and served until 1942] tells me that it will be so extensively used, because of the growth of civil aviation during these two years, that already we must begin to plan other subsidiary airports for Washington as we must do throughout the nation.

"This airport and many others which we hope will follow will draw free men freely to use a peace-time implement of commerce which, we hope, will never be converted to war-time service."

Two weeks after the dedication ceremony, the President laid the cornerstone of the administration building at the 729-acre airport. The new $15,000,000 airport was a pilot's dream and one of the largest in the world. Private and transport planes no longer had to risk disaster attempting to land on the crowded and dangerous old Hoover Wash-

Dedication of the Washington National Airport in 1940

ington Airport, and what the U.S. would have done without the airport during the Second World War is not possible to conceive.

Some 200 other airports, vital to national defense, were constructed under the direction of the CAA by 1941, including LaGuardia in New York. Approximately $200 million had been appropriated by the federal government through public works or work relief programs since 1933 for these airports.

Soon after we were sworn into the authority, we arranged a meeting with the Air Transport Association, the organization of all commercial airline operators, in Chicago. Our entire program agenda was to see what could be done to restore and develop confidence in air transportation so that the airlines would have the business they were entitled to.

At that time there were many accidents. The Air Transport Association had no business because people had no confidence in their mode of transportation. When I made transcontinental flights, I would be the only passenger aboard.

Our goal at the conclusion of the meeting was to have an accident-free year—something that had never been done in any form of transportation. I am sure the people left the two-day meeting feeling that they were out to accomplish the impossible, but everyone was determined to do just that. Everyone went home to lay out his own program—to see what could be done to tighten up and improve safety measures and restore confidence. And because of the efforts of all, we went not only a year, but seventeen months free of accidents to passengers, bystanders, crews, and employees of all descriptions.

This indeed was one of the greatest achievements in the history of transportaton—accomplished without shackling air transport with unnecessary and useless regulations. It was not accomplished by sacrificing services the airlines offered to the American people. Quite the contrary. During the first twelve months our common carriers flew more than 87 million miles. That is equivalent to flying ten times around the world at the equator every day of the year. It was 16 million more miles than had been flown in this country in any preceding year.

The accident-free months were accomplished because of the painstaking devotion to duty, the meticulous attention to detail that the people who manned our airlines displayed in their daily work. No praise that we could have devised would have been more than they deserved.

The anniversary of our first accident-free year was truly a happy one. Two hundred and eight commercial airlines carrying about three thousand passengers were in the air as the anniversary came. Two minutes after the anniversary hour, we in the authority began to celebrate: using over 30,000 miles of teletypewriter circuits that disseminated hourly weather reports, we dispatched a message in code, "NOTAM [meaning "notice to airmen"], Heartiest congratulations to all airline, civil aeronautics authority and weather bureau personnel upon completion of an entire year of airline safety. This is one of the outstanding achievements in the history of transportation." The message was retransmitted by radio to the 208 planes and copies signed by the captains of the planes were then distributed among passengers having their breakfast in midair.

At the end of our accident-free year, I was serving as chairman of the CAA, having been appointed on April 17, 1939, when Ed Noble became under secretary of commerce, and on this truly exciting day I received a letter from President Roosevelt which I read in a nation-wide broadcast from Salt Lake City. It read, "Will you please extend my heartiest congratulations to every last employee of the air lines—be he field boy, pilot, or president—and to your own personnel in the Civil Aeronautics Authority. Looking behind this record, in which we can all take pardonable pride, we find it has been achieved through cooperation and teamwork between the personnel of the air transport lines and workers in the federal government. I trust that this cooperation may continue with like satisfactory results through the years ahead."

Colonel Charles A. Lindbergh wrote to me, saying, "It seems clear that the airlines have passed their period of infancy and youth, and now demand their place among the mature transport systems of the world.

"I know of no one who would have dared dream ten years ago of a safety record in 1939 of over 800 million passenger miles without a fatality. Such a record is truly a milestone in the history of aviation."

The praise didn't stop there. Later the National Safety Council sponsored a Commemorative Award Dinner at the Mayflower Hotel in Washington and presented the CAA and commercial airlines with the Commemorative Safety Award.

Obviously the CAA had made great strides in civil aviation. But there was still another area in which aviation was dragging its wings. In 1938 the U.S. had no education program based around aviation. We had fewer than 5,000 military pilots and 1,000 military airplanes. The Army Air Corps had one training base, Randolph Field, San Antonio, Texas, which could turn out 500 fliers a year. The navy had a base at Pensacola, Florida, with a similar capacity.

In the civilian area we had 9,732 aircraft, including some 400 air transports, and a total of 21,118 certified pilots, many of whom had let their certificates expire.

It was my feeling that national defense called for the training of more pilots, so in 1938, shortly after I took office, I originated a program to increase the pilot population by teaching thousands of students to fly. In this way, I felt, aviation would get into the vocational training system, and fixed-base operators, who would sponsor flight training, would have a chance to make a little money. It would thus give first-aid to defense and a stimulus to postwar industry.

Through Hopkins I got the ear of President Roosevelt, and on December 27, 1938, he announced to a press conference that he had approved my plan to boost the private flying industry by annually teaching 20,000 college students to fly. He said it would be an experimental program, financed by $100,000 of National Youth Administration money and would involve 330 young men and thirteen institutions. It was called the Civil Pilots Training Program (CPTP).

With the help of Dr. Ben D. Wood, director of Collegiate Educational Research at Columbia University, we began to equip colleges and universities to teach a 72-hour ground course in their science classes. Experienced flying schools gave the 35-50 hours of flying instruction. All across the country fixed-base operators experiencing financial difficulties were put to work training fliers. Dean Brimhall, my partner in the Utah-Pacific Airways, joined me in the CAA and was especially helpful in working with the fixed-base operators in establishing flight-training programs. Later, a small research unit was organized under Dean's direction to establish better tests to find out more about the physiological and psychological makeup of pilots.

Training in the pilot program was open to graduate and undergraduate students between the ages of eighteen and twenty-five. They had to be U.S. citizens who already had an elementary knowledge of physics. The colleges were permitted to charge up to $40 as a laboratory fee, $20 of which went for a $3,000 life insurance policy and $10 for a physical examination. The CAA paid the college $20 and the flying school $270 to $290 for each student accepted in the program. Students were selected on the basis of health, aptitude, and scholarship.

Purdue University was the first of the thirteen colleges to get started with fifty students; soon after, the University of Minnesota started students flying on aircraft equipped with skis. The first pilot to start flying, Emmet Hammer of West Liberty, Ohio, took off from the University Airport on February 6, 1939. Probably the most famous graduate of the program, however, was John Glenn, the first U.S. astronaut to orbit the earth. He soloed in 1940 as a CPTP student in Muskingum College, New Concord, Ohio. Some other pioneering colleges, selected because they had established courses in aeronautics, were the University of Michigan, University of North Carolina, Georgia Institute of Technology, University of Alabama, North Texas Agricultural College, Pomona Jr. College, University of Kansas, San Jose State Teachers College, University of Washington, and New York University.

By the end of the first semester, 95 percent of the 313 students had passed their ground and flight tests and were awarded their private certificates. There were twelve dropouts and one fatality. A student in a midwestern university failed to recover from a spin and was killed.

From the beginning, the armed forces were consulted on each step of the program's development and many high officials of the air services gave constructive help in laying out the original controlled courses. Both the army and the navy assigned flight officers in close liaison with the program as it advanced. We were not in competition with the armed forces for students, instructors, or equipment. In fact, thousands of the trainees volunteered for and were accepted into the army and navy.

In an appropriation hearing on the program in 1940, Brigadier General Jacob E. Fickel, assistant chief of the Army Air Corps, commented, "There are three bottlenecks in training for any large number of combat pilots. One is the matter of instructors for primary, basic, advanced, and specialized training. Mr. Hinckley's program will increase the number of instructors almost immediately for primary training. The next bottleneck is equipment, and the demand for high horsepower planes will be increased under this program. The third is in the matter of facilities. Every airport in this country will be used by Mr. Hinckley's program. I think that is why we should build this reservoir of private pilots up, if possible."

At the same hearing, Captain George D. Murray, U.S. Navy Bureau of Aeronautics, testified: "I think the Navy's problem is going to be very greatly simplified and our program will be accelerated by using the trained civilian pilots that are produced in the CAA."

However, there was criticism of the program, and on some days we felt like footballs in a rough game. Oddly enough, though, some of our worst headaches came from our own people. Congressional opinion was sharply divided (on partisan lines) on the value of the program, with some calling it New Deal warmongering. It was denounced as a boondoggle and a waste of public funds, a fraud. J. Edgar Hoover, director of the Federal Bureau of Investigation (FBI), has his men investigate some of the more vocal critics, and reports on these individuals were sent to me. It was in this way that I first became acquainted with this prestigious man, but I saw him a number of times later—usually at the race tracks. Hoover was always with his associate Clyde Tolson, who, because of his love for racing, had a horse named after him. It was said that when the man Clyde Tolson was at the track, the horse Clyde Tolson never lost the race. However, I know of one exception. One day, Steve Early (the President's secretary), Tom Morgan (president of Sperry Corporation), and I were guests of Victor Emanuel (the head of AVCO, one of the early conglomerate corporations) at Laurel Race Track, and we sat in a box adjoining that of Mr. Hoover and Mr. Tolson.

Mr. Emanuel's horse was entered in the race, but because of the legend, Clyde Tolson, the horse, was favored. The legend didn't stand true that day. I laid a moderate bet on Mr. Emanuel's horse and left the track with more money than I ever won before or since at a race track.

In the colleges, opinions varied as to the value of the CPTP. Ernest K. Wilkins, president of Oberlin College, in a letter to congressmen and college administrators, said that, although he was in favor of maintaining a strong national defense, the program of the authority seemed to him to be "ill conceived and unsound." Richard C. Foster, president of the University of Alabama, one of the thirteen institutions in which the demonstration phase of the program operated, said, "So many details of the President's plan are still undetermined, no opinion can be formed regarding it."

Favoring the program was Reverend Robert I. Gannon, president of Fordham University, who said, "Fordham University has always believed in preparedness. That this must now include aviation is obvious and the government plan for training civil aviation cadets while still in college is a further refinement of the sound old ROTC idea." Rufus D. Smith, provost, New York University, also expressed a favorable view: "The Civil Aeronautics Authority program for flight training will be of definite value to our students. However, the full value of this program cannot be determined until the experimental period is completed."

There is no doubt how students felt about the program; hundreds applied for the thirty to fifty slots allocated each school in the first year. And the general public also reacted overwhelmingly in favor. The Gallup Poll reported in the New York *Times* on January 20, 1939, that 87 percent of those queried heartily favored the plan. The survey showed those under thirty years of age approving by 91 percent; ages thirty-one and over, by 85 percent.

If a poll had been taken later that spring, the percent of persons favoring the program would have been even higher. Germany attacked Poland and began to remap the rest of Europe. Peace in the world was past history. Fearing for the defense of his own country, President Roosevelt asked for the first congressional appropriation to aid the Civil Pilot Training Program. He said, "In cooperation with educational institutions, it is believed that the expenditure of $10,000,000 a year will give primary training to approximately 20,000 citizens."

It was not, however, until after six months of foot dragging, and then hectic footwork, that the Civil Pilot Training Act became a law, on June 27, 1939. But instead of the $10 million the President had requested, $4 million a year was authorized—enough to train 9,885 private pilots and insure refresher training for 1,925 instructors during the 1939-40 scholastic year.

As soon as the funds were available, the CAA went to work, and by October 1939 there were 404 colleges offering training. In my own state of Utah, the following colleges participated in the program: Branch Agricultural College, Cedar City; Snow College, Ephraim; Utah State Agriculture College, Logan; Weber College, ogden; Carbon College, Price; Brigham Young University, Provo; University of Utah, Salt Lake City; Dixie Junior College, St. George.

Each college selected its flying schools, and these were then examined by CAA inspectors, who made sure that one airplane of not less than 50 horsepower was available for each ten students. Practically everything with wings on it—if privately owned—was utilized, including two-place Stearmans, Taylorcraft, Aeroncas, Monocoupes, and Piper Cubs. After completing his thirty-five to fifty hours, the student didn't graduate as a finished flyer; he could handle an airplane only under normal conditions and could execute a few simple maneuvers, such as wingovers and loops. However, unlike many military cadets who before CPTP didn't even know the proper names for airplane parts, he was not unprepared to go into the military.

The CPTP during this period wasn't only for students. One part of the program also specified that at least 5 percent of the total authorized flight courses be allocated to young persons not in college. Later, in 1940, the figure was increased to 7 percent and the program gave 700 flying scholarships to seventy communities. Eventually the figure was more than tripled.

Ground school for these noncollege youths was under the supervision of local civic groups and was taught at night six hours a week for twelve weeks. The $10 cost to participants included textbooks. There was no limit on ground school enrollment, but one instructor was required for every fifty students in flight training. Only those between the ages of eighteen and twenty-five were eligible for flight training, which was awarded, after a competitive examination, to the top ten in the class.

Women were also included in the program. Four women's colleges participated, and at other colleges co-eds were accepted in a ratio of one to ten. In the noncollege program, women enrolled in the ground schools competed with the men for enrollment in flight training. (The CPTP increased the number of women pilots in the U.S. from 675 in 1939 to nearly 3,000 in July 1941). The war put a halt to this, however.

In three months in 1940 the German war machine had crushed Denmark, Belgium, Luxemburg, and the Netherlands and was surrounding Paris. On May 16, 1940, President Roosevelt, in a dramatic appearance before a joint session of the House and Senate, asked for $1 billion for defense and an air force of 50,000 airplanes. At that time all the U.S. factories were manufacturing was 12,000 a year, and close to half of those planes were sent abroad. So criticism over the President's request increased by leaps and bounds. Even when manufacturers expressed confidence that they could produce the planes, the skeptics asked where the pilots would come from.

Congress, finally aware of the immediate need for more pilots, came up with the answer, and in the cause of national defense, $37 million was allocated to CAA for the fiscal year 1941. (The initial request for CPTP had been $33 million.) Some 15,980 students were enrolled in the new programs, in addition to 15,000 nonstudents. Training centers, college and noncollege, totaled more than 900. On January 1, 1941, CAA records showed 63,113 private pilots, and a year later the number passed 100,000—almost entirely because of the CPTP. And all this was carried out smoothly, despite a major governmental reorganization of the CAA.

"Air Conditioning" America

To be air-minded is not enough. Something more is needed if the U.S. is to be a nation on wings, which it is surely going to be. This and succeeding generations must become what I call "air-conditioned."

—Robert H. Hinckley

The Civil Aeronautics Act was one of the most awkward pieces of legislation creating a new agency in the history of government. The authority actually consisted of nine men—five who were considered the authority and who acted on routes and rates and everything of a quasijudicial, quasilegislative nature; a three-man Air Safety Board; and an administrator. These were three autonomous divisions, none of which was clear on its specific assignments. As a result, the inherent problems that confronted us as a new agency were intensified by friction, particularly within the Air Safety Board, and everyone was kibitzing on what everyone else was doing in order for each to meet what appeared to be his responsibility.

We realized that amendments to the legislation were sorely needed, but just as we were putting together proposals that would make the act functional, the Budget Bureau completely reorganized the agency "in the interest of increased efficiency and economy." (For five months the Administrative Management Division of the Budget Bureau had made a study of the authority at the request of President Roosevelt.)

The reorganization placed the authority within the framework of the Department of Commerce, where the authority would have a closer relationship with the important reporting services of the Weather Bureau and the essential air navigation chart service of the Coast and Geodetic Survey—plus representation at the cabinet table.

In the reorganization plan the Weather Bureau was brought into the Commerce Department from the Department of Agriculture, a step Ed Noble and I had strongly recommended since taking office in the authority. The Weather Bureau had been under the auspices of a governmental agency as early as 1869, when a bill was introduced in Congress authorizing the secretary of war to take meteorological observations at army posts and to issue warnings for the northern lakes and seacosts. In 1870 the Army Signal Services was designated to continue with these duties.

So by 1891, when public and congressional sentiment leaned toward civilian control of the weather organization, the major phases of a national weather service were well established, including general weather forecast and special warning services, publication of climatological summaries, and research. Soon after, the service was transferred to a newly created Weather Bureau, under the Department of Agriculture. A hurricane-warning service was also organized.

It stayed in the Department of Agriculture because weather reports were developed primarily for farmers. However, because of the growth of aviation, we thought the reports should be developed for flying and every other purpose; this way, not only would farmers get better weather reports than ever before, but people in populated urban areas and in coastal regions would get more accurate warnings of tornadoes and hurricanes.

Transferring the Weather Bureau to the Department of Commerce was one of the real accomplishments of the whole reorganization plan, for aircraft reconnaissance and radar marked a major advance in the warning system.

In the reorganization, the five-member authority (which had received widespread praise by this time) remained an independent Civil Aeronautics Board performing the basic regulatory functions, and it continued to appoint and control its own personnel and submit its own budget. The function of investigating accidents was transferred to the board, which unlike the Air Safety Board, was not helpless to take positive steps toward preventing the recurrence of accidents. Unlike the Air Safety Board, the Civil Aeronautics Board was given the power to prescribe air safety rules, regulations, and standards and to suspend or revoke certificates after hearings.

The several highly paid positions on the Air Safety Board were eliminated, and the administrator of Civil Aeronautics, who was to report directly to the Secretary of Commerce, was made independent of the board and was given most of the spending and enforcement powers which formerly were at least nominally supervised by the authority.

The reorganization of the CAA by the Budget Department caused a furor both in government and within the industry; it was a shock and surprise to everyone. Fifteen hundred airline pilots sent a "Lobby to Save Lives" to work on Capitol Hill. Their prime argument was that when civil aeronautics supervision had previously been under the political control of the Department of Commerce, the supervision was inefficient and many an airplane crashed. (Prior to the establishment of the authority in 1938, the Post Office Department, the Interstate Commerce Commission, and the Department of Commerce all had charge of civil aviation in varying degrees.)

Employees were demoralized. They didn't know what would happen next, and CAA offices were filled with rumors that this or that official would resign in protest of what was going on.

Newspaper and aviation magazines reported that congressmen refused to reject the reorganization plan to make it possible for the President to "save face" against the rising tide of public and press opposition to killing CAA independence. Under the leadership of Senator Pat McCarran of Nevada, the foes of the reorganization could muster only thirty-four votes, whereas two weeks earlier at least sixty-five senators had committed themselves to support the independence of the authority. The issue was strictly political.

I was on the West Coast on agency business in June 1940 and was told of the reorganization over the telephone by my secretary, Roseanna McQuesten. Immediately I instructed her to pack up my belongings in the office and ship them home; I wouldn't return to Washington. Within a short time I received a call from Hopkins and another call from a member of the White House Staff, who asked me to return to Washington and discuss the matter fully. Eventually I did meet with Hopkins and the President, and together they convinced me that it would be impossible to turn this thing back at that time. They admitted that we had made the original Civil Aeronautics Act work—at least amicably—regardless of how awkward the act creating the authority had been, and they asked me to accept the post of Assistant Secretary of Commerce for Air, insisting that I more than anyone else could put the pieces back together again and make the new reorganization work.

So in June 1940 I was promoted to assistant secretary of commerce for air—in charge of the Civil Aeronautics Administration, the Weather Bureau, the Coast and Geodetic Survey and the Civil Pilots Training Program—at a salary of $9,000. It was a promotion at a reduced salary. Colonel J. Monroe Johnson, Assistant Secretary of Commerce for many years, was nominated to the Interstate Commerce Commission to make way for my appointment. And I requested that Colonel Donald Connolly, who had been so successful as an army engineer in various capacities in WPA and subsequently as administrator of Southern California, be appointed by Preident Roosevelt as administrator of the Civil Aeronautics Board. Roscoe Wright, former head of WPA information, was selected as director of the information division of the CAA, and Bert Oakley, who had been working in the navy, became my secretary-"confidential assistant." (Bert had been called to my attention by my brother E. C. Hinckley, who employed Bert when E. C. was safety engineer of the old Ironton Plant between Springville and Provo—the beginning of Columbia Steel in Utah. In 1942 he accompanied me to New York when I left government to join Tom Morgan in the Sperry Corporation. At one point, after I left Sperry, I asked Bert if he would be interested in going back to Utah to help Clarissa run the automobile business. But his career with the large corporation seemed too promising and exciting, so our direct association ended. But our personal relationship continued over the years).

Shortly after these appointments were made, criticism spread like fire. *American Aviation,* July 15, 1940, stated: "With efficiency and organization at the lowest ebb in the history of government regulation and promotion of civil aviation in the U.S., the storm-tossed Civil Aeronautics Authority, hitherto as independent as a government agency could be, moved into a 'dark era' in complete control of former Works Progress Administration 'New Dealers' and 'reformists' whose apparent original objective was the firing directly or indirectly of most of the old line veterans who were part of the Bureau of Air Commerce prior to the creation of CAA.

"It is reliably known that Hinckley is very much on the spot. The White House is watching the CAA closely and still is smarting over the unexpected controversy raised by the reorganization plans with which the President was obviously not very familiar. If the CAA doesn't work out smoothly in Commerce, the blame, according to informed White House circles, will fall on Hinckley since the White House is having troubles enough of its own without adding more aviation battles."

The magazine went on to say, "Rumblings are being heard in Congress. There is still much to be told of the behind-the-scenes activity which brought about the unexpected reorganization. Whether Hinckley will be able to ride out the storm and get his house in order is still debatable but there are not more than one per thousand in Washington who would give him an even chance. The damage, as observers see it, already has been done."

There was little doubt that we had turbulent flying ahead of us, but as assistant secretary of commerce for air, I was appropriated the overwhelming portion of Department of Commerce monies and with the threat of war, we had a large job to do.

Though Hitler's armies failed to knock out Great Britain, in 1941 they conquered Yugoslavia and Greece (which Italy had attacked after entering the war against France in 1940), then marched into Russia. With the world crisis nearing our own shores, the President gave me permission to once again build civilian airports, this time, however, with the approval of the army and navy—so that the airports would be placed strategically for military defense purposes. And in May 1941 I left for England with Major Lucius Clay, assistant to the administrator of Civil Aeronautics Authority and an army engineer, to examine British airport and satellite field programs. Together we visited many of the important air bases and landing fields to learn about the war requirements of the day and to determine what changes and improvements should be made on comparable airfields at home.

One site we had selected for an airport was in Westchester County, New York, a location my good friend Fiorello H. LaGuardia, New York City Mayor, was bitterly opposed to as it was in an area over which he had no jurisdiction. LaGuardia's contention was that the airport would contaminate New York City's water supply and then we'd have a "hell of a mess." To discuss this "horrible thing," the mayor arranged a breakfast meeting with me in Washington. I took Mayor Clay to the meeting in LaGuardia's suite.

We ordered breakfast, and LaGuardia, while he proceeded to shave, asked me "what the hell" I thought I was doing building an airport in Westchester County without researching the matter fully. I told the mayor the project had been properly researched.

He said, "By whom?"

"The Army Engineers," I replied.

"The Army Engineers stink," he said. At this comment I could see the hair bristle on the back of Mayor Clay's neck and he moved to the edge of his seat.

"Well, Mayor," I responded, "I could say the Office of Civilian Defense which you and Mrs. Roosevelt direct also stinks, but it wouldn't mean anything, and our relationship wouldn't benefit by my saying it."

By this time Clay had gotten so angry, he headed for the door, and I followed him. I expected to hear from LaGuardia that afternoon, but only did he not call that day; he didn't call until sometime later. In fact, I didn't hear from him until he read in the newspaper that I was leaving government service to join the Sperry Corporation. Then he called, and asked me to come to his office, where upon my arrival I was kept waiting until he had finished the day's appointments. Then he said, "Come on, Bob. We're going home." Home was Gracie Mansion.

When we arrived, the mayor poured us both a drink and then said, "Why did you do that to me, Bob."

I answered, "Why did you do that to *me*? You made me look like a juvenile who hadn't done his homework." With that, the mayor began to cry, and it wasn't until he'd had a good cry and a few more drinks that we got our relationship back to a normal basis and became the good friends we had been. Later the mayor and I together selected the site for New York's second airport, Idlewild, whose name was changed to Kennedy National Airport after the death of the President.

Our war readiness didn't stop at building airports. In the summer of 1941, training pilots for military service became the prime purpose of Civil Pilots Training, and despite their protests, women were no longer accepted. A military pledge became required of all boys in the CPTP, and all-male classes were started with 16,000.

Just when this group was about to graduate, the bombs fell on Pearl Harbor, December 7, 1941, bringing the U.S. into the war, and the CPTP ceased to be a civilian enterprise. On December 13, 1941, President Roosevelt declared that all pilot training facilities of the CAA were to be "exclusively devoted to the procurement and training of men for ultimate service as military pilots, or for correlate non-military activities."

The name of the program was changed to the CAA War Training Service.

Immediately after the declaration of war, all CAA resources were devoted exclusively to the needs of the army and the navy. Trainees were sent to different schools to learn the procedures adapted to the different techniques of the two services, and the age limit of the trainees was dropped from 19 to 18. Married men were also accepted if their dependents had other means of support.

In the summer of 1942 the War Training Service began operating on seven different flight levels—elementary (240 hours of ground school and 35 to 45 hours of flight training); secondary; cross-country; link instruction; instructor course; flight officers; and liaison pilots. Not only did we become the principal suppliers to the Army and Navy; we also provided instructors to the Royal Canadian Air Force, which was having great difficulty getting its pilot training going. Through meetings with Captain Homer Smith of the Royal Canadian Air Force and air attache to the Canadian Embassy, I arranged to furnish them instructors for training. This arrangement ws established on a friendly, unauthorized basis, and it was continued as long as was necessary.

It was through this activity that I met the famous Billy Bishop, the stocky, blue-eyed air ace of the First World War whose daring exploits gave him every possible decoration for valor and a dazzling reputation. In 1917 he single-handedly destroyed four German planes preparing to take off for their morning's work. During the Second World War, Hollywood producers were trying to get Bishop to make a film of these First World War exploits.

That summer the number of pilots in the CPTP had increased from 25,000 to 45,000 in the elementary program and from 10,000 to 20,000 in the secondary program; at the same time, the navy called upon the CAA to provide 20,000 pilots during that fiscal year, 18,350 of whom would enter combat service. The army, on the other hand, eliminated the CAA's function of precombat training for military airmen and assigned to it the task of instructing only 13,350 students, all of whom were destined for noncombat duty. Because of this, thousands of enlisted men marked time until places could be found for them in the army's own air schools. On government pay they walked the streets or lounged in hotel lobbies.

In addition to this waste, only 3,338 CAA training planes were being utilized, leaving 14,139 training planes available but not employed.

The War Department had no comment on these figures, but Richard L. Stokes, Washington Correspondent of the St. Louis *Post-Dispatch*, did. In the July 5, 1942, edition of the paper he wrote, "From the start CAA has based its policy on utilization of commercial airfields, known as fixed bases and numbering about 600; and of colleges and universities, of which as many as 700 have been enlisted from time to time. The latter supplied students of superior quality, teaching staffs for scientific branches of aviation and ready-made classroom, dormitory, restaurant and amusement facilities.

"Under the current program, it is alleged a considerable volume of these resources will go begging, while the Army yields to the intoxication of building a throng of 'Hollywood' air schools, vast and ornate, which are said to consume inordinate quantities of critical materials, especially steel and cement. Contracts for such institutions, costing from $3 million to $5 million each, are announced almost daily. They are all brand-new and complete with flying fields, housing quarters, classrooms, cafeterias, recreational facilities. Few of them, the prediction is, will be turning out pilots before the end of 1942 or beginning of 1943."

The reporter went on to explain that at a meeting of army officials and CAA officials on January 1, 1942, Major General H. H. Arnold, chief of the Army Air Forces, took the position that the war demanded full use of all the country's pilot and mechanical training facilities, both military and civilian. Even this, it was indicated, might not satisfy total requirements. General Arnold's stand was endorsed on February 21, 1942, in a letter from Secretary of War Henry L. Stimson to Secretary of Commerce Jesse H. Jones.

When Stokes' story came out in print, an authorized spokesman for the Army Air Force replied, "If the Civil Aeronautics Administration doesn't stop squawking, the Army will take 'em over, lock, stock and barrel."

In answer to the gentleman, I said, and was quoted in the newspaper, "We should be in favor of the army taking us over if we thought that would win the war a minute sooner. We don't believe it would. And we are not squawking. We are merely pointing out, in a temperate manner, that this is a total war; that this country's utmost resources will not be too much; and that a substantial proportion of CAA facilities is not being used."

A short time after the article appeared, an emissary from the Air Corps visited me and said if I would bring the CAA into the Army Air Corps, I would be made a full colonel. I asked what was the rank of the officer who had sent the proposal. When the emissary told me he was a major general, I said if he would make me a major general, I would consider his proposal. Of course, he scoffed at the idea, but I emphasized that I would not bring the CAA into the Air Corps and have someone who knew nothing about it tell me what to do.

That was really the end of my ability to serve effectively during the war in the Department of Commerce. After war was declared, the military was of course supreme. The civilian agencies were pushed aside. Whatever the military wanted, it got.

So, after much contemplation, I resigned as assistant secretary of commerce for air that year to accept Tom Morgan's long standing invitation to join the Sperry Corporation in New York. I had decided that there I would be more useful in the war effort than I possibly could be in government, because everything I did in government was eclipsed by the military.

William L. Clayton, deputy federal loan administrator and later special assistant to the secretary, was appointed by Jesse Jones to succeed me.

In December 1942 recruiting stopped and the enlisted reserve became a closed pool in the War Training Service. A month later, in January 1943, however, the Army Air Force did a turnabout and assigned the WTS to establish two divisions—one to train reservists as instructors for the Army Air Forces at the Central Instructor School at Randolph Field, and another for elementary instruction of the army's huge reserve of prospective combat officers. About 14,000 students a month were given the ten-hour course at colleges selected by the air force.

That spring the number of WTS schools was down to 350, and on January 14, 1944, the instructor training was discontinued. In August the navy participation ended when that service reached its goal of fliers, and by the end of the year, the entire WTS was phased out. However, praise for the program was boundless.

E. E. McKaughan, president of Aviation Enterprises, Incorporated, Houston, Texas, said, "The program as a whole is undisputedly the most wonderful and outstanding thing that has happened to civilian aviation."

George E. Haddaway, editor of *Southern Flight* magazine, wrote, "We don't believe anyone can show us any federal project of the last eight years that produced so much good for so little money expended."

My friend Ben Wood, director of Collegiate Educational

Research at Columbia University, wrote to me in a letter of January 21, 1946:: "Not enough time has yet elapsed for people to understand or appreciate the incalculable contributions you made to winning the military war and saving the world from the bestialities of Hitlerism. Perhaps it is mathematically impossible to calculate the ramified contributions of your CPT to the war effort, and it is certainly impossible to estimate precisely the full and ultimate benefits of your pioneering ideas and implementations in the related fields of "air conditioning" the people so that they could successfully fight an air-strategy war and build and maintain a militant peace in an air-age world.

"As you foretold long before Pearl Harbor, the airplane made the quick 'air-conditioning' of our people necessary to survival in the war, and made the 'world-conditioning' of the minds of men everywhere essential to the maintenance of any semblance of peace based on justice and good will.

"We need some more of the kind of pioneer thinking that developed the CPT and the air-conditioning programs."

It was Dr. Wood in 1942 who had helped me to "air-condition" America—to put persons in a state of readiness to do something about aviation and not just feel strongly about it—by presenting flight principles and practices in high schools. In 1939 only 130 of the 28,000 high schools in the country were teaching aviation at all. In September of 1942, under Ben Wood's direction and with the help of the Macmillan Company, whose publishing plants broke all possible records in producing eighteen volumes on the air age, we introduced aviation in all its preflight aspects into more than 14,000 public, parochial, and private high schools which had enrollment of 250,000 pupils. And in that same September 210 high school youngsters began learning to fly.

Here's how it all happened. CAA consultants and the U.S. Office of Education asked colleges and universities to organize teacher training institutes (Harvard was the first to respond), and the CAA gave ground-school syllabuses to high school teachers. The two approaches prepared approximately 4,000 men and women to teach preflight aeronautics when the school year began.

While the "Air-Conditioning Project" was in full flight, CAA lowered the minimum age to seventeen and selected twenty-one high schools at which the CPTP trial flight course would be taught. Each school was given a quota of ten trainees, and 210 boys signed up for the course. Later, because of the untiring efforts of Dr. Wood and other educators throughout the country, aviation-consciousness filtered down into the elementary schools. A brochure, "Education for the Air Age," sent out in 1942 by Allyn & Bacon, a Boston textbook publisher, carried an outline of study from the first grade through the eighth.

The War and Sperry

Ask yourself, "What can I do to shorten this war?" By doing this, thousands of lives may be saved, and ironically no one knows whose lives those may be.

—Robert H. Hinckley

I had not been with the Sperry Corporation long and was just getting my feet on the ground with this great company when I received a letter from James V. Forrestal asking if anything would tempt me into coming back to the "Washington flypaper" with him again.

At this time his request seemed impractical as far as I was concerned, certainly because in my previous years in government I had practically exhausted my personal income trying to properly represent the government on the salaries that were paid. However, I found it difficult to say no to the man, for I had great respect for Forrestal. An unusual man—talented, dedicated—he would later give his life for his country.

I first met Jim Forrestal when I was assistant secretary of commerce. It was the routine of Jesse Jones, secretary of commerce and head of the Reconstruction Finance Corporation, to spend the morning working at the Department of Commerce and the afternoon working at the RFC. Jones would come into my office, usually in the morning, and ask if there was anything he could do to help. If there was, I never hesitated to tell him, and if he undertook a task requested of him, he always came through.

Serving under him was a happy experience, which didn't stop at the end of the day. Once the work was done, it was Jones' custom to hold a sort of open house in his RFC office. So, after 5 p.m., when the sun was over the yard arm, so to speak, all in government who were his friends would congregate in his office, where we would exchange information about what was going on in government in the various departments. Because it was not statutory to pour liquor in government buildings, I don't think Mr. Jones ever poured. He just made it available.

It was at one of these gatherings that I met Forrestal, who was then serving as under secretary of the Navy. While in this post he helped build the United States Fleet into the largest in the world. In fact, in 1954, the Navy named a class of aircraft carriers, the "Forrestal," in honor of him.

When Congress passed the National Security Act in 1947, putting all the units of defense into one agency, Forrestal was appointed the first U.S. Secretary of Defense, which I thought made a lot of sense, as he had worked his heart out to bring about the unification of the armed forces, and in my opinion, had done it better than anyone else could have done.

But with the election of Harry Truman in 1948, Forrestal's efforts were discounted. Louis Johnson was chairman of the Democratic National Committee and had been responsible for Truman's campaign—fundraising and so on. Of course, Truman won the first election pretty largely by himself, even though almost no one, with the exception of Clarissa, thought he would win.

He won, and the request Louis Johnson made of the newly elected President was that he be appointed Secretary of Defense. Truman responded, and Forrestal was forced to resign.

After Louis Johnson was sworn in, some of his personal friends had a reception for him. I was there and Jim Forrestal was gracious enough to attend. He left office with his chin up.

Forrestal left this jollification meeting early, and I followed him out. I will always remember what he said to me at that time. He said, "Bob, do you think it would have been otherwise if you had joined me when I asked you to?"

That was a hard question for me to respond to. I didn't know the answer either.

I had first met Tom Morgan, president of Sperry Corporation, at the World's Fair in New York. Tom, a warm, friendly fellow, well liked by most, was a member of a party of Mayor LaGuardia's friends who attended the dispatch of Pan American Airline's first mail flight to Europe. I think my part in the ceremony, representing the CAA, was sending the pilot on his way with God speed, and while he was in the air, talking with him over the radio.

Tom and I later became better acquainted, and as the war developed, and as he became more and more aware of my part in war preparation, he became one of the great supporters of everything we were doing in the CAA.

When I finally joined Tom as assistant to the president in 1942, the Sperry Corporation and its subsidiaries—Sperry Gyroscope Company (U.S.), Sperry Gyroscope Company (England), Ford Instrument Company, Incorporatd, and Vickers Incorporated—were unique and powerful contributors to the war effort. Their basic strength was in the development of new products, although they already had a foundation of commercial and military aircraft and marine instrumentation and gunfire-control apparatus.

Sperry Gyroscope in this country and in England developed and manufactured commercial and military aircraft equipment and marine navigation equipment and various gunfire-control devices. Ford Instrument's business was 100 percent on naval-gunfire computers (using precision gears, not electronics). Vickers's business was the development and manufacturing of hydraulic devices for the precise control of heavy equipment, for example, the positioning of naval guns in response to the direction of Ford's computers, or the hoisting of heavy ammunition from the hold of a naval ship to the guns that would fire it.

None of these companies were new. Sperry Gyroscope U.S. was formed in 1910 by the renowned inventor, Elmer A. Sperry, to manufacture one product, the Gyro Compass, an instrument which, without error, indicated true north. The instrument revolutionized the science of navigation and gunfire control. The first installation of the Gyro Compass was made in the U.S.S. *Delaware* in 1911. On board the *Delaware* at the time was Tom Morgan.

Sperry Gyroscope's counterpart in England was established in 1915, as was Ford Instrument. Vickers—America's largest manufacturer of oil hydraulic devices—was established in Detroit in 1921.

The Sperry Corporation was not formed until 1933, and then only as a holding and management company for operating subsidiaries that were entirely independent of each other.

Just prior to World War Two, in 1937, Sperry, one of the early conglomerates, had total sales of $15 million. In 1942, when I went with Sperry, sales were about $220 million, and during the two years I was there, sales jumped to about $425 million—more than twenty-eight times the 1937 amount. But with this explosive growth came a myriad of new problems. I was added to the management to help solve these problems.

One of the first problems I worked to solve was this: with the increased volume of business, the corporation's profits, based on current prices and rates of profits, were higher than the management and board of directors considered desirable in time of war. So we took the initiative and proposed to the government reductions in prices and profits on equipment sold to the armed forces.

This voluntary act saved the government and taxpayers about $100 million and produced much long-lasting good will between Sperry and Washington. (This action was a forerunner to the Renegotiation Act of 1942, which allowed the government to retroactively recover excess profits on defense contracts.)

The second problem I faced was the shortage of manufacturing facilities within the corporation. Even with the tremendous expansion of our own facilities, we were unable to handle the gigantic demands for Sperry equipment. To solve this dilemma, at the same time we proposed the voluntary price reduction, we offered royalty-free licenses to other manufacturers to make and sell to the government Sperry-developed equipment.

As a consequence, twenty-six companies such as General Motors, General Electric, Emerson Electric, Ford Motor Company, Chrysler, Briggs, IBM, and Electric Auto-Lite were granted licenses, and Sperry people helped set them up in production.

These companies shipped more than a half-billion dollars worth of Sperry developed equipment. The elimination of royalty payments offered the government substantial savings. We recognized then that this action would generate future competition for Sperry, but we knew too that it was necessary to help win the war.

Another problem brought to my attention while I was at Sperry was in the area of personnel—an area that naturally attracted me.

In the war economy the shortage of people constituted one of Sperry's most pressing problems, corporation wide. Not only was employee turnover tremendous, but we had to develop training programs for people who had never seen the inside of a factory—for women, for minorities, for older people—anyone who could use his hands.

There were also the problems of getting people to and from work and of providing basic employee services and benefits. And the draft situation complicated many of our programs. We would no sooner get someone trained than he would be drafted—or would volunteer, to escape the draft. Competent executives, too, were drawn into the military maw. With this happening, I had no choice but to fill the vacuum, the approach (as always) being to find and hire the most competent "people" executives (no easy task in those days) and let them put their expertise to work at the operating level (no simple task for the best of executives). And these jobs were complicated by the very nature of Sperry.

As I said, the company's primary strength and contribution lay in its ability to develop new devices; its production facilities could not possibly accommodate the flow of new products that came out of the research laboratories. No sooner would the production of one device get smoothly under way, than the Armed Forces would tell us to put some new product on the line. Thus, while meeting the new assignment, we also had to help some other company get set up to complete the first assignment.

This happened time after time. Naval compasses were given to Chrysler. Automatic pilots for aircraft were given to Jack & Heintz. Revolving belly turrets for B-17s, with their Sperry gunsights, were given to Emerson Electric. New products were phased into Sperry manufacturing, such as the A-5/S-1 autopilot-bombsight combination, the MK-14 gunsight for naval antiaircraft guns, a central station gunfire-control system for B-17s and B-29s, an automatic control for land-based antiaircraft guns, computing gunsights for aircraft, and a little later, radar. And so on and so on.

These constantly changing programs imposed a gigantic burden on the company's manpower planning and deployment function, and they continued to plague Sperry throughout the war. However, by working closely with the operating people, I was able to manage the chaos pretty well.

Another area brought to my attention was public relations. I recognized that the day would come when war contracts would dwindle, when Sperry would have to move into civilian products. When this time came, a good name and reputation would help Sperry be successful in any field it decided to enter.

Doing something about my conviction was not easy, however. Sperry's management had always been loathe to talk about the company's objectives and accomplishments; in fact, few members of the management understood that any institution, public or private, exists only by public consent. But in spite of this built-in bias, I was able to sell the management and board of directors on embarking on a corporate communication program to both the public and the employees.

The theme of our advertising program was that Sperry's equipment, good as it was, merely supplemented the efforts of the GIs, making it possible to defeat the enemy with the loss of fewer lives.

Naturally, with this theme the program was a high success, especially with the Armed Forces, and it continued to be the basis of the company's communication efforts. In reading the ads of other defense contractors during the war, it seemed they were trying to claim they were winning the war all by themselves.

Another activity that absorbed a good deal of my time and energies while at Sperry was that of Washington liaison. I kept my apartment at the Mayflower Hotel and spent an average of at least two days a week in Washington informing members of Congress, the Internal Revenue Service, the Armed Services, the Selective Service, the War Production Board, the Defense Plant Corporation, and numerous other governmental agencies how Sperry Corporation had grown and describing its numerous services.

This was probably my most valuable service to Sperry Corporation. Having served in government for many, many years, I knew the pressure points, and in hurly-burly wartime Washington this was a necessity.

Postwar Contract Settlement

Every time history repeats itself, it does so at a higher price.
—Author Unknown

In 1944 I was still in New York with the Sperry Corporation, and Clarissa (when she wasn't in Ogden running the automobile business) and I were living in a penthouse apartment we had been fortunate to rent furnished at Two Sutton Place South at the east end of 57th Street, overlooking the East River. We were able to obtain this apartment because the people who had occupied it were afraid the Germans would start bombing New York once they cleaned up England. We had no such fears and moved in as soon as we were shown the place.

It was there that James Francis Byrnes, director of War Mobilization, called to tell me I was the director of the Office of Contract Settlement, which had been created by the Contract Settlement Act.

I laughed and asked him if he knew any other good jokes, but quickly learned that Byrnes was dead serious, and so was President Roosevelt. So I met with Byrnes and the President several times and told them again and again that it was unfair to bring me back into government since I had served so long and had exhausted my personal means to live in Washington. The salary of the director of the Office of Contract Settlement was one-fifth my salary at

Sperry.

It was no use. The more I talked, the less they listened, and I was forced to take the job. When I say forced, I mean the war was still on, my children were highly involved in the war, and I could do no less. Robert was in the Eighth Air Force with my good friend General Jimmy Doolittle and had led the first daylight bombing mission over Berlin. John was in the infantry in Germany, and Paul was in West Point. Betty and her husband, Preston P. Nibley (who had been frozen into a industrial job; none of the armed services could enlist him), were in the Yukon Territory, Canada, where throughout the war Preston worked for Standard Oil Company of Alaska, which provided fuel for U.S. planes and supplied fuel to Russia and American allies.

So, on August 1, 1944, I was nominated by President Roosevelt to be director of Contract Settlement. Despite the cut in salary, however, Clarissa's reaction to my decision was positive. Clarissa was a good woman; she was my

Judge Harold W. Stephens swearing in Robert Hinckley as director of Contract Settlement. At right: John M. Hancock and James F. Byrnes

woman, my wife, and she supported me in every way. When people would ask her what she thought of my rash maneuvers, she would say, "Oh Hinckley's like Mayor LaGuardia. Hinckley runs to government like LaGuardia runs to fires." (The New York City mayor invariably attended all the fires he possibly could in the city).

During World War II, war procurement in the United States was well over $3 billion. Shifts in the tide of warfare, changes in terrain and tactics and the development of new weapons and supplies necessitated the constant revision of war material procurement. American factories and shipyards were called to meet production schedules previously thought impossible. The result: In 1943-44, the government was forced to terminate contracts with corporation after corporation. This was one of the key problems the nation faced in its transition from war to peace. Although the practice of terminating military contracts at the convenience of the government was as old as the Civil War, never before had the volume been so great. As an unknown author wrote, "Every time history repeats itself, it does so at a higher price."

We had no uniform guidelines. In World War I the War Department had authorized, but never required, the use of a termination clause in its contracts. Therefore, no uniform clause or procedure evolved. In World War II, however, the problem was too immense to ignore, and termination clauses developed in several fields. The War Department initiated a Cost-Plus-a-Fixed Fee Contract in 1940. It contained a provision that the government would assume the obligations and commitments of the contractor on termination of the contract. The Navy Department also established termination articles for use in its contracts, as did the other major procurement agencies—the Maritime Commission, the Reconstruction Finance Corporation, and the Treasury Department. It was during this time that the principle of settlement by businesslike negotiation was initiated. The idea was to settle a contractor's termination claim through compromise and adjustment—the same as businessmen do—rather than to insist upon a complete detailed pre-audit in every case.

Unfortunately, the problem was not solved by the development of these articles. The procedures and requirements of each procuring agency, as well as their views on allowable costs, were unstandardized and unfamiliar. The need for uniformity of termination procedures soon became apparent, and in 1943 the army and the navy took the first step to draw up a joint termination clause. However, it was described as "too cumbersome and detailed for practical use" and had to be abandoned. Only when pressure from not only the government, but from industry, increased did all the procurement agencies get together to discuss the establishment of an interagency committee to bring about the badly needed uniformity and practicality.

The impetus for this was provided by Mr. Byrnes, who had left his position as a justice of the United States Supreme Court (to which position he had been appointed in June, 1941) to assume the functions of "assistant President," taking on all the administrative tasks relating to the war that the President was too busy to handle.

Byrnes had told President Roosevelt that unless he could be used in some productive way in the administration, he would go home to South Carolina and enlist in the war. So, on October 3, 1942, he was appointed director of Economic Stabilization, a job from which he resigned in May 1943 to become director of War Mobilization.

On November 12, 1943, with the cooperation of the principal contracting agencies, Mr. Byrnes set up the Joint Contract Termination Board and made investment official John M. Hancock its chairman. Mr. Hancock had been a partner in Lehman Brothers for many years and had served in high executive offices at Jewel Tea Company, Underwood Corporation, Sears Roebuck and Company, and many other corporations.

In his office Byrnes also created a war and postwar adjustment unit that was headed by Bernard M. Baruch, a long-time governmental adviser associated with Mr. Hancock since 1942, when both had been appointed by President Roosevelt to serve on a fact-finding committee on synthetic rubber. Mr. Baruch had been chairman of the War Industries Board in World War I, economic adviser for the American Peace Commission, and in 1922 a representative of the President's Agriculture Conference.

Together Hancock and Baruch collaborated in writing the "Report on War and Postwar Adjustment Policies," later known as the Baruch-Hancock Report. They included in it the Uniform Termination Article and a sixty-day plant-clearance policy. The article emphasized the need for "fast, fair and final" settlement of war contracts. This was immensely significant not only to assure the continued successful prosecution of war, but also to avoid the bankruptcy of industry in the transitional and postwar periods. The article was the only part of their report enacted into law in the same manner they had recommended. After thorough review, Congress passed the Contract Settlement Act, effective July 21, 1944, to "provide a comprehensive statutory basis for the solution of contract settlement problems."

The act, which created my office, was based on four fundamental principles which substantially governed all its provisions:

1. To prevent mass business failures and widespread unemployment, termination claims of all war contractors had to be settled and paid fairly and speedily.

2. Contractors' plants had to be cleared of unwanted inventory and equipment within sixty days after proper request.

3. Interim financing, up to a high percentage of the contractors' claims, had to be made available within thirty days of application.

4. The government, in settling and paying termination claims, had to be protected against waste and fraud.

Under the legislation creating the Office of Contract Settlement, I could have employed thousands of people to do the work for all the contracting agencies, but after studying the act, I decided to keep the process of terminating contracts as simple as possible. To do this I insisted that each contracting agency be responsible for the settlement of their own terminated contracts. What the Office of Contract Settlement did was establish uniform accounting procedures for every contracting agency. Our office did not decide what contracts should be terminated, nor did it settle any claims. These were the responsibilities of the contracting agencies. Our function was on the policy level and was aimed at insuring that the rules governing contract settlement were simple, uniform, and fair to contractors and to the government.

My experience with the Sperry Corporation helped me here, for Sperry had contracts with almost every contracting agency in government, especially those participating in the war effort. I remembered that prior to the enactment of the Contract Settlement Act, when the various agencies would come to Sperry to settle a terminated contract, their procedures were so varied that it was difficult to believe that they were all working for the same government.

Delay was inevitable. When Byrnes was prompting me to take the office, he told me that the day after Pearl Harbor had been bombed, the Supreme Court considered a suit brought by Bethlehem Steel involving a claim for $12 million arising out of World War I. Byrnes couldn't tolerate such delay; he left the court and joined Roosevelt in the war effort.

As director of the Office of Contract Settlement I had the specific responsibility for investigating terminated settlements and the interim financing activities of the contracting agencies, and for promoting the training of personnel for the two processes. This training was achieved through a variety of programs, including university courses in termination problems.

The first course was inaugurated at the University of Pennsylvania in the spring of 1944, and during the next fifteen and a half months, sixty classes were held and more than 2,600 students—representatives of contractors and professional firms and governmental agencies—delved into legal and administrative matters and problems relating to accounting and inventory and property disposition.

A "Contract Settlement Training Guide" describing several types of training, from brief talks to technical sessions on accounting, was prepared by an interagency committee and printed by the Office of Contract Settlement. This pamphlet was used by teachers who conducted training sessions.

The Smaller War Plants Corporation also issued a Contract Termination Memorandum to its fourteen regional and ninety-three district offices to make sure that contractors' representatives were fully aware of termination problems that could arise. To further reach small and medium-sized contractors, the ABC Course, a four-hour elementary training class, was initiated as well. In the basis course, three instructors played the roles of the contracting officer, the governmental accountant, and the property-disposal man. When the program ended in October 1945, more than 6,000 government employees and 32,000 representatives of more than 22,000 firms had "learned by doing."

Those questions too technical to be dealt with in the ABC Course were answered in the XYZ Course, initiated in June 1945 for contracting accounting personnel.

I had two other principal responsibilities as director of Contract Settlement: collaborating with the Smaller War Plants Corporation to protect the interests of the smaller war contractors in getting fair and speedy settlements, and decentralizing the administration of termination settlements and interim financing. In carrying out these responsibilities, I consulted with and advised the Contract Settlement Advisory Board, made up of representatives of the main procurement agencies. With the assistance of these representatives and my own staff, we did well in a short time.

At the outset I said I would do the job with fewer than 100 persons. As it turned out, my office staff, including secretaries, typists, a chauffeur, errand people, as well as prominent accountants and other financial experts, at no time exceeded 78. Two of these persons were George D. Bailey and Frank E. McKinney.

George D. Bailey, a senior partner of Ernst & Ernst of Detroit, was one of the great accountants in the U.S. at the time we were organizing the Office of Contract Settlement. One day I called him and asked him to join me in Contract Settlement. After he had explained why he could not, I asked him what I would have to do to pry him loose— and following more discussion, further persuasion, and indications, not only of my earnest desire, but also of my real need for someone of his caliber to set up the accounting procedures, he finally agreed to come.

Bailey, who operated with me as a dollar-a-year man, was a great force, and we became lasting friends. He worked with Captain J. Harold Stewart in setting up the general accounting procedures.

When I was setting up the Office of Contract Settlement, Frank E. McKinney was established in New York City, where he was working with contractors in army projects. Marriner Eccles and Larry Clayton had become familiar with his excellent record in this work and as president and chairman of the board of the Fidelity Trust Company in Indianapolis, and they recommended him to me. In my office in the Sperry Corporation in the RCA Building in New York, McKinney and I discussed the possibility of his joining me in the Office of Contract Settlement—an offer he said he would take under consideration. Later he reported that General Carter was reluctant to release him. But that didn't stop me.

When I had demurred in becoming director of the Office of Contract Settlement, I had told President Roosevelt that anyone worth his salt was already employed in government and doing all he could to win the war. His response was that if I had difficulty getting anyone I wanted to join my staff, I should let him know, and he would get him for me. I didn't go to Roosevelt over the McKinney matter, but I did visit the under secretary of war, Robert Patterson, and related to him what the President had said—adding that I was sure he would agree with me that the President was far too busy to be bothered with this kind of problem.

Patterson said, "Leave it to me." I did, and soon McKinney joined me as assistant director of the Office of Contract Settlement with the responsibility of arranging what became known as "T Loans" (Termination Loans)—loans that might become necessary in terminating and settling contracts and getting contractors back to peacetime work in the shortest time. McKinney, with his natural good humor, was a great source of support, a great help in the office.

Other members of my staff included Roger L. Putnam, deputy director in charge of plant operations; Edward H. Foley, Jr., general counsel, who was assisted by Seymour Sheriff; Captain J. Harold Stewart, accounting, who was assisted by Weston Rankin, George N. Farrand, Gerald Maxfield, Edward B. Smith, and Kenneth C. Tiffany; Raymond T. Bowman, progress and statistics; John F. Thomas, property disposal, assisted by James K. Ebbert; Walter F. Wiener, public information, assisted by Nettie Duskis. Martin Taitel was my special assistant; E. J. Madill, administrative assistant; H. Chapman Rose, secretary to the advisory board.

The process of contract settlement, once the termination notice was issued to the contractor, followed a fairly regular pattern. The contractor stopped work and told his subcontractors to do the same. An inventory was taken of the contract materials and work in process. The contractor prepared his claim, showing his own charges and the cost of settling the claims of his subcontractors. (In October 1944 the Office of Contract Settlement gave "blanket but revocable authority" to all contractors to settle claims of less than $1,000 where subcontractors retained or disposed of all inventory. However, the Contract Settlement Act permitted the direct dealing between the government and subcontractors where it would expedite settlements.) The claim was then submitted to the contracting agency, which reviewed it and negotiated a settlement.

Fast, fair, and final. That is how contracts were to be settled. I concluded that this meant fair to the contractors as well as the federal government. My friend Lindsay C. Warren, Comptroller General of the U.S. and responsible only to Congress, thought these contracts should never be paid until they were pre-audited. The Contract Settlement Act did not provide for such pre-auditing, and I didn't intend to be bound by the Comptroller General's traditional method of operating. If I had, we never could have settled these things fast, fairly, and finally and still have done the major portion of the Contract Settlement work, as we did, in less than two years.

At the outset of taking over the office, I spent much time with Warren, trying to convince him that no matter how he felt, he should try to understand the feelings of General Brehon Somervell, with whom he was constantly arguing. Somervell was in charge of all procurement for the U.S. Forces, and to him it was a matter of saving thousands of lives to get ammunition, despite its cost, when it was needed. Warren thought Somervell was wasteful in his method of operation, while Somervell was trying to win the war at the earliest possible moment.

I had a hard time convincing Warren that General Somervell, in his own way, was trying to prosecute the war successfully as much as Warren was through his cautious scrutiny of all federal expenditures. And then I had to convince General Somervell that Warren was also a good citizen, that all he was trying to do was to keep government expenditures to a minimum. Both gentlemen, both my friends, finally warmed up so they were on speaking terms with each other.

We had another thing in Contract Settlement we called "team settlements," which amounted to one agency's settling on behalf of a number of agencies that had terminated contracts. This was particularly important at the end of the war, when masses of contracts had been terminated with large maufacturers like Sperry. The agency having most contracts would settle for all agencies. This action provided settlement of contracts fast, fairly, and finally.

In all, more than 320,000 prime contracts were terminated and settled during and subsequent to World War II with little trouble. The Office of Contract Settlement had to intervene very seldom. As of March 31, 1947, only 103 appeals involving termination claims had been taken to the office's Appeal Board, and more tha 50 percent of these were settled to the satisfaction of both parties.

While the contracting agencies and the contractors were reaching an agreement, disposition of the property involved in the termination was arranged. It was sold to a third party, retained by the contractor, or transferred to the government. It was the government's right to take title to the termination inventory, but this action was taken only where critical items were involved. The general policy was to take title to as little of the property as possible.

To govern the disposal of all governmental surplus, the Surplus Property Act was passed on October 3, 1944, creating the Surplus Property Board to supervise the disposition of termination inventories. The sixty-day plant clearance policy—which stated that when a contractor requested an inventory clearance, the government had sixty days to complete the clearance—turned out to be one of the board's best aids to reconversion. By March 31, 1947, plants had been cleared of $7.4 billion of inventory—94 percent of the total plant clearance task, which was estimated to involve $7.9 billion of inventory. Of this inventory, about 56 percent had been sold or retained by the contractors; 16 percent had been retained by the contracting agencies; and 28 percent had been transferred to War Assets Administration for disposal as surplus property.

Interim financing, for the period between termination and the final settlement, was the final step in the contract termination process. Without such funds, many factories would have lain idle, their employees been jobless, and the contractors gone bankrupt.

To keep contractors on their feet through the interim period, private financing was made available, as were partial settlement payments (from the government) and guaranteed T-Loans, which could usually be obtained within thirty days after termination. Application for a T-Loan had to be reviewed by the contractor's local bank, then the district Federal Reserve Bank, and then the local liaison officer of the government procurement agency.

Normally the government guarantee was 90 percent of the loan, but occasionally it went as high as 95 percent. Although only a small portion of the interim financing was handled through T-Loans—the maximum amount was $30 million in December 1945—their availability assured industry of money once their contracts were terminated.

So, from the beginning of war production through March 31, 1947, some 320,000 prime contracts were terminated, involving canceled commitments of $65.7 billion, about one-fifth of the total cost of the procurement program. And there was no unemployment, because there was no interim between war and peace work.

In June 1961 Mr. Baruch, who was really responsible for the Contract Settlement Act, said, "The accomplishment of the Office of Contract Settlement was the greatest, smoothest and most efficient job done by any governmental agency.

"Before they started on it, the papers were saying there would be 10 million unemployed in the transition from war work to peace work. As a result of the work of this Office of Contract Settlement, there was no unemployment during the transition. No one knew why, or who brought it about because it was done so smoothly."

When I left the Office of Contract Settlement on February 1, 1946, to join my friend Ed Noble in another pioneering adventure—the founding of ABC Television—I was succeeded by H. Chapman Rose. Roger L. Putnam followed as director on October 1, 1946, and held the office until the functions of the director were transferred to the secretary of the treasury on December 12, 1946.

Ed Noble, cofounder of ABC Television

My dear friend and beloved President left government service nearly a year prior to my departure. On April 12, 1945, Franklin D. Roosevelt lost consciousness forever. It was a tragic and sad day.

It was Steve Early, the President's secretary, who broke the news to the wire services, and within minutes bulletins were flashing on wire machines in every newspaper office in the country. John Charles Daly, a young news commentator at CBS-Radio was editing copy in the newsroom when he was stunned by the report. Within seconds he had interrupted the show *Wilderness Road* to bring to the American public the special, earth-shattering bulletin. Other newsmen were doing the same, but in America's city streets there was no need for radios or newspapers. The tragedy was on everyone's face; people openly wept as they walked along their way.

I had just returned that day from a trip to England with H. Chapman Rose, where we had gone to see what our problems would be at the end of the war. I was in my apartment at the Mayflower Hotel when a member of my staff called to ask if I knew the President was dead.... I was as stunned as the rest of the world.

Shortly after 7 o'clock that night, Harry S. Truman was sworn in as the thirty-third President of the United States.

My association with Truman had begun long before this eventful night, when he came to Washington in 1934 as a senator from Missouri and was a member of various committees. Our friendship had been helped along by Robert E. Hannegan, also a Missourian, who in January 1944 became chairman of the Democratic National Committee. In that capacity Hannegan had promoted Truman for the vice-presidency as a replacement for Henry Wallace, prior to Roosevelt's campaign for election to a fourth term. One term of Wallace seems to have been enough for everybody. Thus, Hannegan was perhaps entirely responsible for Truman's election as vice-president and subsequent succession to the Presidency.

During his period as President (1945-53), Truman occupied a suite at the Waldorf next to mine. This happened because when General Douglas MacArthur, supreme commander of the Allied Powers, retired, or was fired by President Truman, in 1951, he took up residency in the Presidential Suite in the Waldorf and never left. He died there. His occupancy made it necessary for the Waldorf to develop a new Presidential Suite. So when the tenant in another suite—34A—died, the hotel immediately redid it into the Presidential Suite. I was living in Suite 34B, which made it convenient for President Truman and me to visit when he came to town.

In the American Broadcasting Company we had an Italian sculptor of great talent by the name of Jock Manton who had become a producer for us because sculpturing was not in great demand. When President Truman became my neighbor in Suite 34A, I thought it would be a good idea for Jock to do a bust of him. The President was agreeable and promised to give Jock all the time he could spare when he was in New York, and when he would leave, we would store Jock's work in my pantry until the President returned. The President was most delighted when the bust was completed and presented to the Truman Library in Independence, Missouri, on its dedication day. Mrs. Truman thought it the best bust ever done of her husband. I think this was because it showed the President with his glasses on. All the other busts that had been done showed him without them.

Harry S. Truman was the same kind of man as President as he had always been as an individual. He was a person of great intellectual integrity, but a person who was a complete realist—right down to earth. He was the kind of person you liked to go fishing with; a person who, even when separated from a friend for a long time, would take up where he left off when the two did meet again. There was no need for getting reacquainted.

After he retired from the Presidency, I visited with him often in New York, but I remember one occasion in particular. Truman had made his usual morning walk with reporters, and one reporter had asked him what he thought of Martin Luther King.

"He's no damn good," Truman replied.

The reporter remonstrated, "But, Mr. President, he was given the Nobel Peace Prize."

"Well, I didn't give it to him," Truman responded.

I stopped by to see Truman the day after the episode, which was in the New York papers of course, and was met at the door by Mrs. Truman, who greeted me warmly as I told her how happy I was to see her, and how I thought it was always better when she was along with the President.

"Well, I wish I could do more," she said. "If I could make those morning walks with him, I probably could prevent some things—like what happened yesterday."

On my resignation from the Office of Contract Settlement, President Truman wrote to me, "Congratulations upon your superior performance of the difficult task assigned to you.

Mr. and Mrs. Robert H. Hinckley, President Harry S. Truman, and Jock Manton

"You laid down the major policies governing the fundamental work of the Office of Contract Settlement with rare skill and foresight.

"The interests of the Government were protected at every stage. The adequacy of your preparatory work was demonstrated abundantly. This is emphasized in the rapidity with which contracts have been settled since the defeat of Germany and Japan and the fact that estimates indicate less tha five percent will be pending at the close of the current fiscal year. For this you have earned the thanks of the nation.

"Having given ten of the last twelve years to government service of outstanding value, you are entitled to return to private pursuits. I am glad you plan to enter the field of radio. The speedily expanding activities in that field, including broadcasting, will afford you an adequate opportunity to exercise your diverse talents."

Television: Its Freedom

No government ought to be without censors; and where the press is free, none ever will.
—Thomas Jefferson

Televison as we know it wasn't really developed until the 1920s, and the first American telecasts on a regular basis didn't start until June 1936. That's when the Radio Corporation of America (RCA), which owned the Red Network (National Broadcasting Company) and the Blue Network, installed televison receivers in 150 homes in the New York City area, and NBC's New York station began broadcasting programs to these homes. The first program was the cartoon *Felix the Cat.*

The first official network television broadcast in the U.S. was on February 1, 1940, when a program from NBC in New York was picked up and rebroadcast by General Electric's station WRGB in Schenectady, New York. About a year and a half later the Federal Communications Commission (FCC) authorized the beginning of commercial television.

Most other countries in the world, with the exception of Great Britain, were totally unprepared to begin television services in 1941, when the U.S. was making regular broadcasts, but then the world crisis put a damper on our televison progress, too. In April 1942, after Pearl Harbor brought the U.S. into World War II, the Defense Communications Board put an end to the construction of radio and television stations, and what televison broadcasting remained began to be used for civil defense purposes such as air-raid-warden training.

It was at about this time that Ed Noble entered the broadcasting picture. As I said, RCA owned both the Red Network (NBC) and the Blue Network. But in early 1943 the FCC changed all that by ruling that no single organization could own more than one network. So, after stripping the Blue Network of all its good programs and all the affiliate stations they could move over to the Red, RCA put up the separate coast-to-coast Blue Network for sale. Established on January 9, 1942, the Blue Network then had 159 radio stations, two and a half of which were managed and operated by the Blue Network Company, Incorporated, a subsidiary of RCA. These were WJZ, New York, a full-time 50,000 watt station; WFNR, Chicago, also a 50,000 watter, shared by Prairie Farmer; and KGO, San Francisco, which operated with 7,500 watts. Most of the Blue Network radio programs originated from these three stations. Televison was barely on the horizon.

Although bidding for the network was active, it had been up for sale for a year and a half before Noble, chairman of Life Savers Corporation, made the highest bid and purchased the network for $8 million in cash. He was the first individual ever to acquire such a large network in an outright sale—although initially he hadn't intended it to be that way. Noble had made an agreement with James H. McGraw, Jr., president of the McGraw-Hill Publishing Compay, to go into this thing with him; but before the deal was consummated, McGraw backed out. So Noble took over the network alone.

Among those Noble was reported to have outbid were the investment banking house of Dillon, Read & Company, the Mellon interests of Pittsburgh, and Marshall Field, Chicago financier and publisher. It was reported in financial circles that Dillon, Read bid $7.8 million for the property. The original asking price was $15 million.

At the time of the purchase, Noble also owned Station WMCA of New York, which he had bought for $850,000 early in 1941, and which he agreed to dispose of when he bought the Blue Network—"in accordance with the policies of the FCC of not having a person own two stations in one city". His full devotion was to the Blue. "I accept fully the responsibility of public service which ownership of the Blue Network will place on me," he said the day of the purchase. "In fact, I regard this responsibility to the people as an elected official sees his responsibility to the public. In every phase of broadcasting—public service, the all-important war service, news, information, entertainment—the Blue will continue to serve its listeners and to increase its service to the nation".

Stating that he was "tremendously impressed" with the network's record of public service, Noble announced in a New York *Times* article (July 31, 1943), "The policies and practices which have been responsible for the network's record of accomplishment will be continued. The officers and executives who have guided the destinies of the Blue Network since its separation will continue at the helm". Mark Woods continued as president and Edgar Koback as executive vice-president. Noble became chairman of the board.

On January 23, 1946, I joined him as vice-president in charge of Washington operations and a member of the board of directors. Prior to this I had branched out into radio ownership with interest in KULA Honolulu and KALL in Salt Lake City. I had also become a stockholder in Universal Broadcasting Company, an Indianapolis AM-FM permittee. However, after the FCC ruled that one person couldn't own minority interests in local stations, in addition to network interest, I gave up my 22 percent interests in the Universal Broadcasting Company, and for a while it appeared I had made the wrong choice inasmuch as the company was sold to Corinthian Broadcasting Company for $10 million.

I had been able to obtain stock in ABC shortly after joining Noble because two of his friends, Roy Larson of

Time magazine and Chester LaRoche, head of an advertising agency in Greenwich, Connecticut, who had been given sizeable amounts, turned the stock back to Noble and because he in turn made 50,000 shares available to me at a very low price. I borrowed the money from First Security Bank in Salt Lake City to purchase the stock, which was never that low again.

I had established a policy about money early in life, when I learned that it takes money to earn money, and that having no money, I had to borrow. But to borrow money a person had to have a credit rating, and I did not. I must have an honest face, or at least make a good appearance or presentation for it has always been possible for me to borrow money—fortunately, I say. Some would say, "It is not right, it's unfortunate; it isn't good manners, it isn't good economy; it isn't logical in any sense of the word to borrow money."

During my life there have been periods where I have been in debt close to a million dollars, and I suppose today I am in debt a few hundred thousand. But because I have been able to borrow money, my net looks good today.

At the time I went into business with Noble, there were fewer than 10,000 television sets in the country, but it was clear that TV would be the major type of broadcasting within a few years, so we moved rapidly to make the Blue hookup a viable third network. The first thing we did was to change the name of the Blue Network to the American Broadcasting Company (ABC), which wasn't easy as there were so many outfits throughout the country—some in communications—called "American." So the change had to be thoroughly researched by our lawyers before we could clear our network of its old name.

It then seemed that the practical thing for me was to obtain some television stations. So I spent my early days at ABC obtaining stations in the major markets—first where the Blue Network had radio outlets. The television stations available were all VHF (Very High Frequency). The low frequency channels were already licensed, and UHF (Ultra-

High Frequency) wouldn't become available until after all the VHF spectrum had been preempted.

I obtained a television channel—channel seven to be specific—in New York, Chicago, Detroit, Los Angeles, and San Francisco—the cities that on the basis of population and business potential were regarded as five of the first six markets. And I did all this without FCC hearings. (We chose channel seven because it was in the middle of all television receivers tuning from channel 1 to 13, so whether the TV set was push button or dial tuned, ABC would have a preferred position. The engineering department was of the opinion that channel seven was superior because there would be less noise on the channel, less possibility of interference from FM stations, less possibility of interference from cochannel television stations, and better transmitting antennas because of the higher frequency. And the channel was available to ABC on a coast-to-coast basis, which meant that television—receiver owners when traveling could always get ABC at the same spot on the dial.)

Whenever I mentioned that I had been able to obtain these stations without a hearing, some of my associates would say, "Well, you got them because nobody else wanted them." I admitted I wouldn't have been able to get them without a hearing if anyone else had wanted them, but I felt entitled to credit for wanting them. Both NBC and CBS have been endeavoring to get five stations in the first six markets, but neither has succeeded yet.

Anyway, on August 10, 1948, our first television station, WJZ-TV, New York, went on the air from the famed Palace Theater on Times Square, where a large part of the initial program, full of variety and comedy and packed with talent and vitality, was picked up. Our ultramodern transmitter and antenna was atop the Hotel Pierre, but nevertheless that night there were line difficulties which threw pictures on local sets momentarily out of focus or off the screen entirely, discouraging our viewing audience.

Despite this, Harry MacArthur, radio editor of the *Washington Star,* wrote on August 11, 1948, "For all the difficulties that plagued the transmission of the premiere of the American Broadcasting Company's new video 'flagship', there was plenty of showmanship in evidence in the programming. There is much to indicate that television set owners are in for some happier times. Television may very easily be, as a matter of fact, the new home of vaudeville that many are claiming it is to become."

Time magazine reported, "The Palaces audience stormily approved every bit of it", and *Variety* magazine commented, "Televiewers have never before seen a show quite matching that one. The video director Paul Mowrey and his crew rate an A-plus for effort and plenty of kudos for over-all performance ... Terrific entertainment. *Billboard* magazine printed, "Sock video ... entertainment on the highest level."

ABC was on its way. Our early programs on WJZ-TV brought life to the black-and-white screen. There was *Hollywood Test*, in which talented young artists took a movie test while talent scouts looked on. Bert Lytell was host. We also broadcast *Three about Town*, the talent trio of Phyllis Wood, Betsi Allison, and Bill Harrington, and *That Reminds Me*, with Walter Kiernan, the weaver of homespun philosophy and droll tales of life on a hundred main streets. Mr. Kiernan interviewed some of his more famous colleagues on the air, including "Uncle Jim" Harkins, radio actor; ex-governor Harold Hoffman of New Jersey, and Tex O'Rourke, swashbuckling soldier of fortune. And there was *Cartoon Teletales*, starring Pinto the Pony, Cletus the Caterpillar, and Alice the Alligator to keep the kiddies spellbound.

ABC's key television station for the Middle West, WENR-TV, Chicago, came into being September 17, 1948, with aother spectacular premiere. A special survey made in Chicago that night between 7:15 and 11:00 showed the channel with a 61.7 rating (approximately 84 percent of the audience). One of the competitive stations, carrying the Chicago White Sox–Philadelphia Athletics baseball game, had a 2.1 rating. (Broadcasting professional baseball games was out of the financial realm of ABC at this time. We would have had to bid one-half of our entire annual budget for these rights). The other competitive station carried the Chicago Rockets-Cleveland Browns professional football game, which rated 9.6.

Variety magazine tabbed that premiere—four hours of entertainment—as "the most impressive television show eyed here to date."

Station WENR-TV's antenna was located atop the Civic Opera Building, 1271 feet above sea level, so the reception was sharp and clear.

Our other three stations also began broadcasting that year—WXYZ-TV, Detroit, in October, transmitting from the Maccabees Building on Woodward Avenue, with an antenna 1,100 feet above sea level; KECA-TV, Los Angeles, in November, transmitting atop Mt. Wilson, 6,000 feet above sea level; and KGO-TV, San Francisco, in December, transmitting from Mount Sutro, where a 500-foot tower brought the total antenna height to 1,360 feet above sea level.

That year we also gained affiliate stations in Philadelphia (WFIL-TV), Boston (WNAC-TV), Washington (WMAL-TV), Baltimore (WAAM-TV), Minneapolis (WTCN-TV), San Diego (KFMB-TV), New Orleans (WDSU-TV), Toledo (WSPD-TV), Syracuse (WAGE-TV), Ft. Worth (WBAP-TV), and St. Petersburgh-Tampa (WSEE-TV).

There was one problem with all this. Having five stations in the first six markets and affiliate stations was like having circus tents and no circus. While we had pioneered televison to the point that we were ahead of all the other networks, we still had only one million viewers. There were not enough television sets in the country to support any kind of programming. With no sets there could be no programming. Programming was expensive at best—horribly expensive if you couldn't sell advertising—and because there weren't enough viewers to sell advertising to, we were in a bind.

This wasn't the least of our problems. In 1948 there were

thirty-six televison stations on the air, and seventy under construction and the stations' signals began to interfere with each other. So, on September 30, 1948, the FCC declared a freeze on the licensing of any new television stations until it had studied frequency allocations and considered problems caused by the apearance of colored TV (it finally came into being in 1956). The freeze wasn't lifted until 1952, and within a few months the FCC had processed a backlog of 700 applications for new stations and had granted 175 licenses. Within a year there were 377 stations on the air and by mid-1954, almost 90 percent of the country had televison coverage. In the early days people used to crowd around department store show windows to catch a glimpse of the televison turned on inside. In 1950 six million persons had sets of their own.

A number of factors contributed to the rapid growth of the televison audience. In the beginning days of televison, most screens measured only 7 or 10 inches (18 or 25 centimeters) diagonally. By the fifties, 21 inch screens were common. At first, most telecasts were live productions or programs made from film, which took time to develop. Also, the equipment and techniques produced pictures and sounds of poor quality. Videotaping began in the mid-1950s, and became a major production method. Videotapes were produced instantly and resulted in almost no loss of quality. This allowed flexibility in program scheduling and made possible such viewing aids as instant replay of sports events.

Reporters of class and quality and their superb coverage of special events also did much to widen televison's appeal. And ABC had a long list of outstanding news commentators, including Elmer Davis, Drew Pearson, Bill Lawrence, and John Charles Daly (who entered broadcasting in 1937, when he was assigned to cover the White House as President Roosevelt was beginning his second term, and in 1953 was made vice-president of ABC in charge of news. We went on to win the Sylvania, Sigma Delta Chi, and *Look* magazine TV awards for our coverage of the 1952 political convention, and the George Foster Peabody and Sylvania TV awards for ABC's 1956 coverage. In 1954 Daly also received the Peabody Award for distinctive televison reporting and news commentary.

Daly became one of my closest friends, as did Elmer Davis, who was thought by many to be a dangerous citizen. Of course, he wasn't. Davis was one of the sanest men I have ever known, and I always believed he was one of the great talents when it came to reporting and broadcasting news and his views. And he was fearless. I think the title of one of the biographies written about Davis after his death was *Don't Let Them Scare You.* That of course was the way he lived. Another title of one of his books or one written about him was *But We Were Born Free.* That was his whole lifestyle. At ABC he started on the daily broadcast basis but then, because of his health, had to be cut back to doing one broadcast a week. Finally he had to stop broadcasting altogether. I saw little of him during his last days because he was having no visitors, but before then I was invited to many functions of the so-called intellectuals at his house—some of which I attended. As a reporter he had no equal.

One of the most outstanding special events covered by our reporters in the fifties was the famous Army–McCarthy hearings, in which Senator Joseph R. McCarthy accused the U.S. Army of "coddling communists," and the U.S. Army charged McCarthy's staff with "improper conduct." The high point of the hearings came when Joseph Welch, the soft-spoken lawyer for the army, and the outspoken McCarthy clashed in an emotion-filled argument that left our viewing audience spellbound. This was the beginning of McCarthy's downfall and ultimate censureship by the Senate, which crushed him completely and finally.

The broadcast of these hearings, under Daly's administration from beginning to end, was the first time such a hearing had been televised completely. Although it was very expensive (we had no sponsorship), it contributed a great deal toward better government and, of course, toward making ABC a broadcast entity.

As Daly's awards show, ABC also covered all political campaigns and party conventions. Of particular interest to me was the 1960 Democratic Party Convention, for I was a close friend of Lyndon B. Johnson, Massachusetts Senator John F. Kennedy's opponent in that convention.

I had become acquainted with Johnson when he was secretary to Representative R. M. Klebert (1932-35), and then when he was elected to Congress from Texas in 1938. At that time he was very close to the administration. In fact, Roosevelt made it a point to use him whenever it was convenient or necessary. We became better friends, and I became well aware of his different moods, when he became a senator in 1948 and when we were both in the broadcasting field. Johnson's personality was determined mainly by the occasion: he could be a "hail fellow well met," and some took it that he was that way all the time—which was not true. If things did not go to his liking, he could be a very disagreeable arm twister; and of course, he never would permit anyone, whatever the occasion, to appear to come off better than he.

In 1960 Johnson was a candidate all the way, but for his own reasons he refused to act like one. John B. Connally, who later became governor of Texas (1963-69), was also a close friend of Lyndon, so he and I met in Lyndon's office (when he was Democratic Whip of the Senate) for many, many days to come up with a campaign strategy. But it was no use. Lyndon's idea of impressing the voters was to stay home and run the store—staying off the hustings, leaving them completely to Kennedy. Neither Connally nor I thought that this was very smart or very good, but Lyndon persisted—right up until the time of the convention in Los Angeles.

The Democratic headquarters in Los Angeles were in the Biltmore Hotel. The Democrats had practically taken over the Biltmore, and of course all the news agencies were trying to get in. ABC had rooms there, I had one, and my old and dear friend Sam Rayburn, Speaker of the House

Robert H. Hinckley and Lyndon B. Johnson

during the war years, had a suite, where I was welcome any time of the day or night.

Rayburn wasn't only my friend; he was Johnson's friend and—much more than that—Johnson's mentor. Johnson didn't make a move before discussing it with Rayburn.

Well, a funny thing happened in Los Angeles. Even though Johnson, up to that time, hadn't been active in his own candidacy for the nomination, he became very active at the convention, and got involved to the extent that he had a debate with Kennedy. This may have grown out of the rumor that Kennedy's health was bad—a rumor ascribed to Johnson. The debate took place, but in my opinion, Kennedy won it hands down. Of course the outcome of the convention was Kennedy on the first ballot, which you could have gotten some reasonable bets on before the voting started. Kennedy was nominated before the roll call ever got to Utah.

After the nomination some old-heads of the Democratic Party, such as Richard J. Daley of Chicago and some of the strong New York leaders, got together and told Kennedy that if he wanted to be elected he would have to have the strength of somebody in the South like Lyndon Johnson. It was because of this advice that Robert Kennedy, John's brother, called on Rayburn and asked him to use his influence to get Lyndon to become the vice-presidential candidate. Rayburn's reply was, "If your brother wants to talk to me, he knows where I am."

It wasn't until John F. Kennedy himself visited Sam Rayburn that Johnson became the vice-presidential candidate.

Unfortunately ABC wasn't as lucky in being able to televise other special events, particularly Senate sessions. In 1954 (the ruling still holds today) television cameras were not allowed in the Senate Chambers, although newspaper reporters were. Because I believe strongly that the press should be the watchdog of government, in August of that year I appeared before the subcommittee on rules of the Senate Committee of Rules and Administration to protest this regulation. I told the committee members that televison was as much an instrumentality for the free dissemination of news guaranteed so wisely by Article I in the Bill of Rights as was the printed page, still or newsreel pictures, or the radio. And it was my contention and conviction that in our newsgathering activities we were entitled to the same free access to governmental news developments as were other informational media covered by the First Amendment.

There had been assertions that televison coverage "Hippodromed" the proceedings, made a "circus" of them, impairing the dignity of the Senate, but I argued that a television camera and sound equipment were incapable of producing any such miracle. The seismograph doesn't cause the earthquake; it merely records it. And no one could say that live televison coverage made President Eisenhower's inauguration less solemn and dignified than it was.

So that there could be no misunderstanding, I told the committee that our insistence on our constitutional rights as a full member of the free press did not mean that radio microphones and televison cameras would be running amok in the Capitol. Actually, I looked for relatively small change in the immediate future. Hearings that stir national interest to the roots were few and far between. Most committee work is careful, time-consuming, almost drudgery. Only occasionally did such a momentous issue arise that people across the country wanted to follow it in every detal.

My testimony, and those of others in the broadcasting field, did little to convince the senators of our right to be in the Senate chambers, however. Even before we appeared, the resolution to keep us out had been endorsed by thirty-six senators. We went into court, so to speak, with more than a third of the jury subscribing to a prepared verdict and sentence before we had been given opportunity to submit testimony.

This policy is unfortunate; the freedom of the electronic media should be extended to the Senate Chambers. Freedom of reporting, in both the printed and the electronic media, is a necessity, for while we have it, there can never be a successful Watergate. Had it not been for the freedom of reporting, the grab for power in the Watergate episode could have been successful. It was only the exposure by the press that eventually brought the Watergate catastrophe to light.

On another occasion I was called to testify for ABC at a public hearing, when televison was charged with causing juvenile delinquency. This time I testified that I could remember when the Model T was charged with juvenile delinquency because it took the kids out of the home. I said television ought to be given a plus for keeping kids in the home so their parents know where they are.

From 1948 (two years after I joined Noble) to 1956, there were a lot of changes within ABC. For example, in 1948 the network made a public offering of 500,000 of its shares at $9 a share, which was sold in two hours. On May 23, 1949, Mark Woods was given a five-year contract as president of the network. But in less than a year, despite the contract, Robert Kintner was made president; Woods, vice-chairman of the board. On February 16, 1953, came the bigget change: the FCC approved our merger with United Paramount Theaters.

Prior to this, several groups had come to Noble wanting to merge with him because he had televison stations in the top markets, and because stations in those markets could no longer be obtained without a hearing, some of which went on for ten years before the FCC made a decison. It was evident that ABC needed more financial help. As a matter of fact, Noble had conferred at length with William S. Paley, chairman of the board of CBS (Columbia Broadcasting System), about the possibility of Paley's taking over ABC and bringing it into CBS. I advised at that time that that could never be brought about because the FCC would not permit it. The merger would cut down competition, and the FCC believed that three networks were viable, could become strong, and that the competition would improve programming and all that. So, the idea of a CBS-ABC merger was discontinued.

Later we were approached by United Paramount Theaters, Incorporated. After lengthy hearings, the FCC—by a vote of five to two—approved our application to merge. We became known as ABC-Paramount Theaters, Incorporated. That was our corporate name; later it was changed to American Brodcasting Companies, Incorporated.

The merger gave us the kind of capital we needed to make bold new strides in becoming an increasingly competitive force in the radio and televison industry—a force helpful to advertisers and sponsors. On the facilities front, ABC was able to embark on a $2 million program to bring super-power televison to our five stations and to plan substantial improvements in our San Francisco televison facility.

Prior to the merger, United Paramount Theaters had

been forced to make certain changes in its corporate setup, one of which was to relinquish the picture-making end of its business. And that gave it the capital ABC sorely needed. However, it continued to own, operate, and lease more than 500 motion-picture theaters. And because of its knowledge of motion pictures and the purchase of new programs, United Paramount became very active in ABC's programming, bringing into the network stars like Sammy Davis, Jr., and Frank Sinatra, which gave us a real boost. We also had the funding to make contracts with Georgie Jessel, Danny Thomas, Ray Bolger, and Walt Disney.

And in 1954 we made an agreement with New Orleans Mid-Winter Sports Associated to carry over the radio and TV networks the January 1, 1955, Sugar Bowl football game. We also entered agreements with four American League and two National League Baseball Clubs to broadcast as many as eight of their games.

An interesting sequence of events took place on the eve of the merger. Haley, McKenna, and Wilkinson was the Washington law firm representing ABC when I joined the network, and it was out of their offices that I worked until I helped my friend Sal Taishoff, publisher of *Broadcasting Magazine,* buy the building at 1735 DeSales Street, formerly the headquarters of the Democratic National Party. (The Democratic Committee had discovered that the building was not big enough when there was campaigning going on, but too big when there was no campaigning. So the Democratic National Chairman, Frank McKinney, who had been my financial deputy in the Office of Contract Settlement, decided to put it up for sale. However, because the building could not be sold at a profit, all bids had to be the same, and McKinney had to choose among them. I suggested to Sal that he put in the standard bid with the understanding that he would also make a substantial contribution to the Democratic Party. This he did, and he became owner of the building. When it was refinished, I moved out of the law offices and took an office on the eighth floor for ABC.) Haley, McKenna, and Wilkinson was a young law firm, in my opinion not completely adequate in representing ABC in all its Washington problems. So I induced ABC to also retain Arnold, Fortas, and Porter—Paul Porter being a former chairman of the FCC and most knowledgeable in all things pertaining to broadcasting and the FCC's mission. I don't think there was another living soul as apt in that area as Porter, who had been a good friend of mine for many years. Some thought my action was on account of that friendship, but it was not in any way. I wanted to retain Arnold, Fortas, and Porter simply to buttress our legal status in Washington.

As far as I was concerned, the only notable thing about the law firm of Haley, McKenna, and Wilkinson was that on the very eve of our hearings when the FCC would determine whether or not to approve our merger with United Paramount Theaters, the firm broke up. Haley went one way, McKenna and Wilkinson the other; and it became my responsibility to decide whom we would select to continue our hearings. I choose McKenna and Wilkinson, and for this they have occasionaly expressed their appreciation, because the FCC became their biggest and sometimes their principal client, and over a period of years has made the firm wealthy.

At the time of the merger, Leonard H. Goldenson was head of Paramount Theaters, Robert O'Brian was vice-president, Walter Gross was legal counsel and vice-president, and Sidney Markley was vice-president. In the main this was a good group, but for some reason, even though Noble as head of ABC was responsible for the merger, they tried to downgrade him by saying they had bought ABC. It would have been impossible for Paramount to purchase ABC, because they could never have obtained FCC approval. It was only on the basis of a merger that the two could have come together.

In 1956, Goldenson, with the support of his group on the board of directors, fired Kintner and assumed presidency of ABC. James Riddell was made executive vice-president, and Oliver Trez was made president of televison. Trez, if he had followed protocol, would have reported regularly to Riddell, but this he refused to do. As a matter of fact, the day he was appointed and the announcement was made at a meeting of affiliates in Los Angeles, he made it crystal clear he would report only to his boss, Leonard Goldenson. (Actually, according to organizational charts, his boss was Riddell.) Well, he made it completely impossible for Riddell to do what he was supposed to, and so Riddell was made vice-president in charge of all West Coast operations, succeeding Earl Hudson. (Hudson, who had resigned from ABC because of poor health, soon passed away.)

I continued to supervise Washington operations and to serve as a member of the board and of the executive committee that set the general policies of ABC. I was always very close to Ed Noble. He was my friend; he trusted me to the point that it was sometimes embarrassing because it seemed I was the only one he trusted. (Of course that certainly was not true.) And friendship continued even after I resigned from ABC in 1965, returning to Utah to become involved once more in my normal pursuits—including politics.

Political Participation

We do not say that a man who takes no interest in politics minds his own business. We say he has no business here at all.

—Pericles

In 1956, planning my full-time return to Utah, I purchased from Robert Kiesel 240 acres of land on the north bank of the middle fork of the Ogden River, three miles east of Eden (population 226), in the central part of Ogden Valley. On the land, which had been a defunct dairy farm, stood the original apple tree. No one would deny it. The property really wasn't good enough to be a farm. It was too rocky, and there weren't enough tillable acres. Nor was it big enough to be a ranch. So, because Eden was our post office address, we named it the Garden of Eden. And there, in 1960, we built our home.

Later I bought the J. Bert Nelson defunct dairy farm, an additional twenty acres, from his brother, and the Eggleston defunct dairy farm across the road west of our home. Then, when Froerer Real Estate bought the Hardy farm to the south of us for subdividing, I purchased all the land north of the middle fork of the Ogden River, increasing my garden to approximately 500 acres.

Of course, I realize I am only the temporary caretaker of the land. My children will inherit it, and their children after them. Then some day, I suppose, some of my descend-

Robert H. Hinckley at his Garden of Eden

ants will get an offer from subdividers or someone else, and they will sit around and think about it, and think about it some more, and then decide they would be "out of their minds" not to take it. And that will be the end of the Garden of Eden.

When I bought the first piece of land, Bob Kiesel told me that if I would get feeder steers in the spring and grass fatten them during the summer, I would be able to sell them profitably in the fall. I tried this for three years and discovered it wasn't true. So, after discussion with knowledgeable persons at the Agriculture College in Logan, Utah, as to what might be done to make such land profitable, I decided to go into the horse business. This was also done in an attempt to find suitable horses for my children.

As I said, the Kiesel property had been an unprofitable dairy farm, so with the help of my old-time friend Ray Ashton, president of the National Association of Architects,

I redesigned the barns and outbuildings, converting the dairy barn into a horse barn, and doing the same with the dairy barn on the Nelson land. We removed the Eggleston dairy barn, a monstrosity between the house and the highway. Then, after thorough research, I began to raise Welsh ponies—a breed big enough for children to ride but gentle enough for little kids to handle. The Welsh Pony is quite unlike the Shetland, which is not big enough for big children and not gentle enough for little children.

The original home of the Welsh Mountain Pony was in the hills and valleys of Wales. He was there before the Romans and, like few other breeds, survived the severe winters when vegetation and shelter were sparse. Even when Henry VII issued an edict that all horses under 15 hands be destroyed, the Welsh were not eliminated. Instead, they flourished because they hid in desolate areas where Henry's persecutors were reluctant or unable to go. Thus, the proud stallions, the bands of mares, and their foals continued to roam over mountains, in ravines, and through rough terrain. The ponies were imported to the U.S. as early as the 1800s, apparently first by George E. Brown of Aurora, Illinois. It was through his efforts and those of John Alexander that the Welsh Pony and Cob (the word *Cob* was dropped in 1946) Society of America was formed and certification for the establishment of a breeder registry was issued by the U.S. Department of Agriculture on July 30, 1913.

By then a total of 574 Welsh had been registered, and the owner-breeder list showed applications coming from Vermont, Ohio, Kentucky, Virginia, Texas, Oregon, Iowa, Massachusetts, New York City, and Canada. Mr. Brown called the Welsh, "the grandest little horse yet produced."

Although interest in the pony dropped during the Depression, in the midfifties many new members joined the society and more ponies were imported. So by the close of 1957, a total of 2,881 had been registered. Over the past decade it has become the fastest-growing breed of pony in America, with an average of more than 500 new owners recorded annually.

When I first inquired about the breed, I became acquainted with Mrs. McKay Smith in Whitepost, Virginia, noted for her ability in selecting and importing stock from Wales and then developing them once she got them to this country. Needless to say, she was one of the leaders in the Welsh Pony business in America. So throughout the years, I bought from Mrs. McKay Smith's stock, until we had developed the largest herd of registered Welsh Ponies, with the best bloodlines, in the West. At one time we had eighty-five of the hardy, spirited, strong ponies. My good friend John Charles Daly jokingly said on one occasion that he was sure one day I would enter one of these ponies in the Kentucky Derby. I knew the horse wouldn't have a chance, but I was sure it would benefit by the association. And Paul Porter added that if I hadn't wanted to withstand the criticism I received when I was building airports for the federal government, I could have run the Welsh Pony Express between the high density markets. That's my friends' thinking for you!

In the course of all this, I began attending the meetings of the Society, later to become its director and then president of the Welsh Mountain Ponies Society of America.

In addition to the ponies I also bought a purebred Arabian mare from the Kellogg Herd in California for Clarissa to ride, and from that mare got some very good foals. Then Robert and his wife, Janice, started getting their own Arabians, and soon, because the market is better for Arabians, we shifted our emphasis from Welsh Ponies to Arabians. As the Welsh pony carries a trace of Arabian blood and crosses well with many other breeds, today we breed the two, coming up with a fine medium-sized horse.

It is these beautiful animals that graze in the fields of the Garden of Eden, which over the years has been the site of may happy family gatherings. One of the most special of these was held on my eightieth birthday. That day my sons unveiled a painting of horses grazing in a field, a painting given me by the Hinckley Institute of Politics and which still hangs above the fireplace in our home.

John also presented me a bound book of "birthday letters" from my friends all over the country, and my granddaughters sang two of my favorite songs, "It Was a Very Good Year" and "What the World Needs Now." Family skits of past milestones in our lives also brought fun and laughter (and a few tears) that day as well.

But the big surprise came when Clarissa appeared in a black silk dress that Grandmother Peel (Clarissa's grandmother) had worn on her fiftieth wedding anniversary. Clarissa had gone down to the basement and had taken the dress and a bonnet, some eyeglasses, and a cane from an old trunk. When she appeared upstairs, her remark was, "Why wasn't I invited to the party?" This was the highlight of the day. I was completely surprised.

There also have been many gatherings of our friends at the Garden. We held a Governor's Day to honor Utah Governor Calvin L. Rampton. There was a day set aside for John W. Gallivan, publisher of *The Salt Lake Tribune;* one for Perry Sorenson, assistant to the president of the University of Utah; one for Gordon Hinckley, a member of the Council of Twelve Apostles of the Mormon Church, and one for University of Utah President David P. Gardner. We were just planning a day in tribute of George Eccles, president of First Security Bank Corporation, when Clarissa suffered a stroke and on August 30, 1973, died, bringing great sadness to the Garden. Clarissa had been my love and partner in all things, and it was she, when I returned from Washington in 1965, who encouraged me to begin another project I had sketched out in my mind. It was a project to upgrade the name of politicians.

While in government I had thought much about the plight of politics and politicians. It seemed that the belittling of politicians was a favorite national pastime. I had been through the depression years, had gone through the New Deal from its beginning with Roosevelt and Hopkins, and had seen people practically on their knees imploring Roosevelt to save them. And he did. Had it not been for his courageous measures and bold moves, the country would have gone communistic for the simple reason that people were in dire need. They had had poverty up to their ears: Communism could be no worse, and the chances were that it could be better.

But after the Depression, when—thanks to the government—the people were back on their feet and some had become prosperous, they couldn't say enough vile things about that man in the White House. This concerned me deeply, and I began wondering what could be done to create more respect for politicians. On a number of occasions I discussed it with my associates, including President Truman, to whom I suggested that because politics is the science of government, we should call politicians "governmenticians." He just laughed, saying that he thought "governmentician" sounded too much like "mortician" and that he would continue to be a politician from Missouri. He said there was only one way to improve public esteem of politicians, and that was to improve the breed.

I agreed with President Truman. To improve politics and politicians we had to select better people to represent us, and to do that, all citizens must participate in government—to become, to some degree, politicians.

After this prelude, I decided to do something definite to get people to participate. In 1965, after I had developed the idea of an institute of politics, the Noble Foundation agreed to match me in a $250,000 fund. Then it was just a matter of deciding where the institute should be established. There was a question in my mind whether or not it should go to the University of Utah, in Salt Lake City, where there was only one Democrat on the Board of Regents (and he a Democrat in name only), or to Brigham Young University, in Provo. (I had been made a member of the University of Utah Board of Regents in 1929 by Governor George Dern and had served three terms; and a short time after this incident in 1965, I was reappointed to a fourth term.) It was through the help and encouragement of Samuel Thurman and Fred Emery of the University of

Utah Law School that I decided to offer the institute to the U. of U. (Previously we had established the Edwin Smith Hinckley Scholarship Fund at Brigham Young University as a memorial to my mother and father.)

I made the presentation to the Board of Regents on a day when they were balloting for recipients of honorary degrees. It so happened that the chairman of the board, who was one of the nominees, was having great difficulty getting himself elected, so the meeting ran overtime. Finally, however, they recessed long enough for me to come in and make my presentation. Afterward John and Robert said I did fine but that no one heard me because the board was so involved in getting this chairman an honorary degree, or in preventing him from having one.

Anyway, they accepted the institute with thanks. We then had the task of setting the thing up and selecting a director. After I had met with a number of faculty leaders and the administration, Dr. J. D. Williams, professor of political science, was chosen for the position, and the institute took a strong step forward. Almost immediately Dr. Williams was sent on a trip across the country to get ideas from all political sources, and we announced in the *Daily Utah Chronicle,* the University of Utah student newspaper, that applications were being taken for Hinckley Institute internships. Four students were selected—the fearless four that ultimately became 600 interns in our first decade. In our first ten years, five of these interns sat in the Utah State Legislature and one on the Constitutional Revision Commission. One was chairman of the Democratic Party in Davis County, and one was administrative assistant to Utah Senator Jake Garn in Washington, D.C.

In 1966 the Hinckley Institute Caucus Room opened its doors and the Politicians-in-Residence Program was inaugurated by Jim Farley, Democratic National Party Chairman during the Roosevelt Administration, and Leonard Hall, Republican National Party chairman during the Eisenhower Administration. The two came simultaneously to the Institute—Farley to tell students about his break with

President Roosevelt over the third-term issue in 1940, and Hall to reminisce about his personal effort to keep vice-president Richard M. Nixon on the ticket in 1956 despite all the protests being made against him.

After their superb presentation, my friends asked me what we would do for a encore, but we managed to fulfill their expectations by bringing to campus many other distinguished guests. Governor George Romney of Michigan visited, telling students that Americans have got to stop looking to government for the solution of all problems and begin to realize the strength in individual citizens and private associations. Senator John V. Tunney of California was another visitor. His session was entitled "The Art of Winning," which meant to him that the practical place for any would-be candidate to begin is through active involvement in the speakers bureau of a highly regarded charitable organization. "In my own case," the senator said, "I became 'Southern California's expert on leukemia,' and spoke to thousands of civic groups who were quite prepared a while later to make the leap from cancer to politics."

The central theme of the 1971 visit of Secretary of the Interior Walter J. Hickel, who broke with President Nixon over matters of conservation and youth, was "The earth is yours: get involved in politics and protect it." Another guest, Senator Mark Hatfield of Oregon, emphasized that winning is obviously important but that what ultimately counts is the lasting good the politician may do for his fellow man and the kind of peace he can ultimately effect with his Master.

Congressman William Anderson of Tennessee, whose real fame was as commander of the *Nautilus*—the submarine to navigate beneath a polar icecap—was at his best with the Naval ROTC midshipmen when he came as our guest to the University of Utah. But he reminded the midshipmen that, in a ratio exceeding a thousand to one, the most important battles in life are going to be won in the smoke-filled room of politics and not in the operation center of a nuclear submarine. "Gentlemen," he said, "also prepare yourself for citizenship." There was also Collin Jackson, the very funny British politician from the House of Commons, who told us, "The thing that makes us in England so really sadis not just that we lost you, but that you learned so little at your mother's knee. After all, we really do have a suggestion or two on how to conduct elections in three weeks' time for less than $60 million—or, let's see, are you now up to $80 million?"

There were others who came to the University of Utah as Politicians-in-Residence, many of whom were my close friends and came as a favor to me.

However, history has not been good to all whose pictures hang in the Hinckley Caucus Room. The Republicans sent us Harry Dent, who pleaded guilty to a misdemeanor in the Watergate incident in 1974. But by and large, the Politicians-in-Residence Program has over the years served a useful purpose in bringing truly exemplary politicians into the student arena and has demonstrated beyond a doubt that in addition to being the most important thing in a democracy, politics can also be honorable.

Many of our guests also participated in the Coffee and Politics Series, another of the Institute's endeavors to keep politics in the scholastic and public eye. The discussion series was hosted by students. The guest spoke only ten to fifteen minutes—the balance of time being used for answering questions. One of the most heated discussions of this type took place during the Middle East Crisis, when a graduate student from Egypt played the role of Premier Gamal Abdel Nasser, a professor played the role of Israel's Premier Golda Meir, two students acted as Jewish and Egyptian representatives, and Dr. Williams assumed the part of the secretary-general of the United Nations and introduced a peace plan. The representatives of the two countries were sharply divided over everything from historical claims to Palestine, through the settlement of Arab refugees, to navigation rights to the Suez Canal—and feelings got so high that at times the Arabian and Israeli students in the audience almost had to be separated. But most of the Coffee and Politics Series were more temperate, as when consumer advocate Ralph Nader was our guest and told students that "in a day and age when the critics contend that American pluralism is dead, I hope very deeply that I have been able to set an example of what the individual citizen and small organized groups can still accomplish in American politics. General Motors knows, do you?"

Nader was one of my favorite guests in the Coffee and Politics Series, not because he was after this specific reform or another, but because—as Hays Gorey, author of *Nader and the Power of Everyman,* describes it—his goal is "an ethic of participatory 'citizenship' not far different from Jefferson's exhortations about 'eternal vigilance.'" That's the theory on which the Institute of Politics was established.

Involvement was our theme when we set up the Hinckley Institute, and during the tense quarter of 1970, the period of the Kent State University student protests over America's involvement in Cambodia, a Hinckley intern by the name of Suzanne Dean realized what an asset we had in the computerized tapes of our students, a computer, and a fascinating program of Utah Senator Frank E. Moss that would identify voting districts of persons whose names you feed it. With these three items a plan was devised to produce a printout of the entire student body in voter districts—the perfect politician's finders tool. So "Participation '74," as the program was called, was able to sell to any political candidate (for under $35) a list of every student in his voting district.

The Institute initiated many other programs to increase student participation. There was the oral history program, in which Americans who either had made history or had seen it made were invited to the Institute. There, before our television cameras, they answered the questions of a panel of interviewers, bringing history to life for years to come. And in 1974, in the wake of Watergate and the ultimate resignation of President Richard M. Nixon, the Institute impaneled a fascinating group of citizens and politicians to write a code of political ethics.

In the summer of 1975 the Institute celebrated its tenth anniversary, fulfilling my utmost dream. Dr. R. J. Snow, associate professor of political science, assistant to President David P. Gardner of the University of Utah, and a former student of Dr. Williams, replaced the resigning director. Three persons to assist Dr. Snow were also named: Dr. Ruth Scott, assistant director for High Schools and Participation Programs; Dr. Armando Navarro, assistant director for Minority Training Programs, and Dr. Ronald Herbenar, assistant director for Internship Programs.

The major Institute programs were continued. Participation '76 aimed at involving literally thousands of students and citizens in electoral politics and campaigns during that critical election year, which featured not only the national race for President and Vice-President but also the reelection campaigns of Utah's senior senator, Frank E. Moss, and of both Utah congressmen, Allan T. Howe and K. Gunn McKay.

In addition, a minority training project, which Dr. Williams had made possible by obtaining a $94,000 grant from the Rockefeller Foundation, was put into action in 1975. The program, designed to interest minority students in political affairs, involved fifteen minority interns, who began with formal classwork that prepared them for subsequent opportunities to serve first as interns in political campaigns, then as staff interns during the regular legislative session, and finally as administrative assistants.

Under Dr. Snow's direction, the Bill Lawrence Internship, in memory of the deceased newsman, was also made available to students, as was the Abrelia Clarissa Seely Hinckley Scholarship for graduate women who would make politics their career. And to expand even further the philosophy of participation, the Institute's programs were extended into area high schools. Previously we had joined with the Robert A. Taft Institute of Politics to offer a special two-week seminar in politics and public affairs for training high school teachers.

Also under Dr. Snow, an advisory committee was organized to direct the Institute, and an annual fund-raising drive was initiated to give prospective politicians the funding needed to participate.

You know, it's funny. One dictionary's definition of politician is, "One who, in seeking or conducting public office, is more concerned to win favor or to retain power than to maintain principles." The *Oxford English Dictionary* defines a politician as a "crude schemer, a crafty plotter, an intriguer" (a definition now obsolete in Britain). Simon Cameron, Republican boss of Pennsylvania in the last century, once said, "An honest politician is one who, when he is bought, will stay bought."

You've heard people say, "Why, I wouldn't touch politics with a ten-foot pole." But, if people don't there will be no democracy.

In the twentieth century many national and international problems confront us. We have a lagging economy, unemployment, diminishing natural resources, farm problems, difficulties in education, civil rights, world trade relations, a world population explosion, poverty, underdeveloped countries, questionable world peace. All these problems and more, because they are political in nature, become the responsibility of politicians. Only politicians equipped with intelligence, integrity, and complete dedication can contribute the best answers to these problems.

We are a democracy. Politics is the lifeblood of democracy. We can, as George Bernard Shaw indicated, have politics without democracy, but we can't have democracy without politics or politicians. That's what democracy is all about. Politics is democracy in action, and as Sir Winston Churchill said, "Democracy is the worst system ever invented—except for the rest."

After serving in government for many, many years, my concern today is not with extremists or the lunatic fringe, some of whom always have been with us. My concern is with the overwhelming preponderance of Americans who believe in democracy and only hope to see it function more efficiently and more responsively to the needs of the day. Political wallflowers don't make our democracy work. What will make our democracy, our politics, work even better, is for all of us to become politicians—to fight for the political leaders we think can best do the job, and further to fight for the candidates that best represent our own political thinking. I agree with James MacGregor Burns, who said, "The cure for democracy, people used to say, is more democracy. A half century of hard experience has shown this cliche to be a dangerous half truth. The cure for democracy is leadership—responsible, committed, effective and exuberant leadership."

That's why I say participation in politics is the minimum responsibility of all citizens.

To mention only world peace—the greatest of our problems: when, as, and if that peace is obtained, it will not be the scientists who achieve it. It will not be the theologians who bring it. It will not be businessmen (unless they be practicing politicians). It will be the politicians. That's why I believe politics and politicians are important. Very important. Most important.

Bibliography

Bishop, Jim. *Roosevelt's Last Year: April 1944–April 1945.* (New York: William Morrow and Co., 1974)

Byrnes, James F. *Speaking Frankly.* (New York: Harper and Brothers, Publishers, 1947).

Charles, Searle F. *Harry Hopkins, Minister of Relief.* (Syracuse, New York: Syracuse University Press, 1963).

Daughters of Utah Pioneers, Weber County Chapter. *Beneath Ben Lomond's Peak: A History of Weber County, 1824-1900.* (Salt Lake City: Publishers Press, 1940).

Final Report on the WPA Program, 1935-43. (Washington, D.C.: U.S. Government Printing Office)

Graff, Robert D., and Robert Emmett Ginna. *FDR.* (New York: Harper and Row, Publishers, 1963).

Hopkins, Harry. *Spending to Save.* (W. W. Norton and Co.: New York, 1936).

Miller, Merle. *Plain Speaking: An Oral Biography of Harry S. Truman.* (Berkley Publishing Corp.: New York, 1974).

Neff, Andrew Love. *History of Utah 1847-69.* (Deseret News Press: Salt Lake City, 1940).

Nichols, Jeanette P. *Twentieth Century United States: A History.* (D. Appleton-Century Co.: New York, 1943).

Sherwood, Robert E. *Roosevelt and Hopkins: An Intimate History.* (Harper and Brothers: New York, 1948).

Strickland, Patricia. *The Putt-Putt Air Force.* (Department of Transportation, Federal Aviation Administration).

Index

Air Transport Association, 77
Alemite Company, 25
Alexander, John, 142
Allison, Betsi, 128
American Broadcasting Company, 44, 117, 120, 126-28, 134-39
American Guide, 59
Anderson, Clinton, 68
Anderson, Nels, 62
Anderson, William, 147
Army Corps of Engineers, 61, 62, 74, 89, 92
Arnold, H. H., 95

Bailey, George D., 113
Barker, James L., 21
Barns, Herbert, 50
Baruch, Bernard M., 109-11, 117
Beadles, W. C., 37
Beesi, Melli, 72
Belmont Park, 72
Bennett, E. C., 37
Bigelow, Archie, 32, 33
Biggers, John D., 67
Bishop, Billy, 93
Blood, Henry, 41-45
Bolger, Ray, 137
Botterill Dodge Dealership, 25
Boutard, Charles, 72
Bowman, Bill, 34
Bowman, Raymond T., 114
Branche, Harlee, 71
Branion, R. C., 46
Brigham Young Academy, 2, 5, 8, 10
Brigham Young University, 1, 2, 21, 84, 145, 146
Brimhall, Dean, 29, 32, 34, 36, 72, 80
Brimhall, George H., 13

Brown, George E., 142
Bryan, William Jennings, 1
Bundy, Arthur, 18
Burns, James M., 152
Byrne, Grace W., 60
Byrnes, James F., 106, 109
Cameron, Simon, 151
Chase, Stuart, 34, 35
Cheeseman, Walker, 29
Chrysler Corp., 26, 27
Chrysler, Walter, 26
Church of Jesus Christ of Latter-day Saints (Mormon), 1
Civil Aeronautics Act, 70, 71, 73, 75, 86, 89
Civil Aeronautics Authority, 70-73, 77-80, 84-90, 93-95, 98
Civil Conservation Corps (CCC), 42, 43, 67
Civil Pilots Training Program, 80-84, 89, 92-94, 97
Civil Works Administration (CWA) 45-47
Clay, Lucius, 62, 91, 92
Clayton, Lawrence, 17, 113
Clayton, William L., 96
Clift, John, 29
Cohen, Benjamin V., 54, 55
Colbert, Tex, 26
Colten, Don B., 5
Columbia Broadcasting System (CBS), 136
Communism, 54, 65, 145
Connally, John B., 132
Connolly, Donald M., 61, 75, 89
Contract Settlement Act, 106, 110, 111, 115, 116
Corinthian Broadcasting Company, 125
Corcoral, Thomas G., 54, 55

155

Creel, George, 60
Curtiss-Wright Company, 26, 27, 32
Cutler, Leland, 60

Daley, Richard J., 134
Daly, John Charles, 119, 130-32, 143
Davis, Elmer, 130, 131
Davis, Sammy, Jr., 137
Dean, Suzanne, 149
Dent, Harry, 148
Dern, George H., 34, 37, 39-41, 63, 145
Deseret, 1, 6
Disney, Walt, 137
Doolittle, Jimmy, 107
Durrant, William C., 25
Dusenberry, Ida Smoot, 10
Duskis, Nettie, 114

Early, Steve, 82, 119
Ebbert, James K., 114
Eccles, George, 30, 144
Eccles, Marriner, 17, 18, 30, 34, 35, 38, 41, 113
Eden, Utah, 140
Emanuel, Victor, 82
Emery, Fred, 145
Farley, James A., 40, 146
Farrand, George N., 114
Federal Arts Projects, 58-60
Federal Bureau of Investigation (FBI), 82
Federal Communications Commission (FCC), 123-25, 127, 130, 136, 138
Federal Emergency Relief Administration (FERA), 44, 45, 47, 48, 51, 53, 56, 68
Federal Reserve Board, 35
Ferry, Hugh, 25, 26
Fickel, Jacob E., 81
Field, Marshall, 124
Fillmore, Millard, 6

Fillmore, Utah, 6
First National Bank, 17
First Security Bank Corporation, 30, 34, 37, 126
Foley, Edward H., 114
Forrestal, James V., 99-101
Foster, Richard C., 82
Franklin, Benjamin, 15
Fretz, Bessie S., 37
"Friedenkers", 33, 35
Fry, Reginald, 25

Gallivan, John W., 144
Gammeter, Emil, 19, 20
Gannon, Robert I., 83
Garden of Eden, 140-44
Gardner, David P., 144, 150
Garner, James, 60, 61
Garn, E. J. "Jake", 146
Gates, Emma Lucy, 19
Glasmann, Abe L., 34, 35
Gledhill Dodge Company, 31
Glenn, John, 80
Golden Gate International Exposition, 60
Goldenson, Leonard H., 138, 139
Gorey, Hays, 149
Grant, Heber J., 2, 3, 49, 65-67
Grant, Jedediah M., 2
Gravelly Point, 74
Greenwell, Darrell J., 34, 35, 44, 51, 67
Gross, Walter, 138

Haddaway, George E., 96
Haley, McKenna, and Wilkinson, 137
Hall, Leonard, 146, 147
Hancock, John M., 109, 110
Hammer, Emmet, 80
Hannegan, Robert E., 119
Harrington, Bill, 128
Harrington, F. C., 74
Hatch, George, 35
Hatfield, Mark, 147

Hay Adams Hotel, 51
Henry, Elizabeth Bacon, 6-8, 10
Henry, Robert, 6, 7
Herbenar, Ronald, 150
Hester, Clinton M., 71, 75
Hickel, Walter J., 147
Hinckley, Abrelia S., 11-14, 20-23, 28, 29, 33, 37, 51-53, 70, 106-8, 121, 144
Hinckley, Adelaide Noble, 9
Hinckley, Adeline Henry, 7, 8-10
Hinckley Dodge Company, 29-32, 51
Hinckley, Edwin S., 7, 8-10
Hinckley, Gordon B., 144
Hinckley Institute of Politics, 143, 146
Hinckley, Ira Nathaniel, 7-9
Hinckley, John S., 29, 30, 37, 51, 53, 107, 144, 146
Hinckley, Janice, 143
Hinckley, Lucian, 5
Hinckley, Paul Ray, 29, 33, 37, 51-53
Hinckley, Robert H., Jr., 28-33, 51-53, 107, 143, 146
Hoffman, Harold, 128
Hoover, Herbert, 22, 33, 39, 40, 60
Hoover, J. Edgar, 82
Hopkins, Barbara Duncan, 53-55
Hopkins, Harry, 39, 44, 45, 47, 48, 50, 51, 53-56, 58, 59, 61-63, 65, 68, 70, 73, 74, 79, 89, 144
Hotel Utah, 28, 34
Howe, Allan T., 150
Howe, Maurice L., 60
Humphrey, Tom H., 50

Ickes, Harold L., 41, 55
Idlewild Airport, 92
Influenza, 28

Jackson, Collin, 148
Jacobson, R. C., 68
Jefferson, Thomas, 1, 123

Jessel, George, 137
Johnson, Hyrum, 63
Johnson, J. Monroe, 89
Johnson, Louis, 100
Johnson, Lyndon B., 132-34
Joint Contract Termination Board, 109
Jones, Jesse H., 95, 96, 99, 100

KALL Radio, 35, 125
Kennedy, John F., 132-34
Kennedy, Robert, 134
Kiernan, Walter, 128
Kiesel, Robert, 140, 141
King, Martin Luther, 121
King, Sam, 24
King, William, 24, 34, 72-74
Kintner, Robert, 136, 138
Klebert, R. M., 132
Koback, Edgar, 125

LaGuardia Airport, 77
LaGuardia, Fiorello H., 91, 92, 101, 108
Lahey Clinic, 65
Lahey, Frank H., 65
Lane, Darrel T., 73
LaRoche, Chester, 126
Larsen, Roy, 125
Lawrence, Bill, 130
Lea Bill, 71, 72
Lindberg, Charles A., 79
Lyman, Richard R., 8
Lytell, Bert, 128

Madill, E. J., 144
Madsen, Charles K., 60
Maeser, Karl G., 2
Manton, Jock, 120, 121
Markham, Edward W., 62
Markley, Sidney, 138
Mason, G. Grant, 71
Maxfield, Gerald, 114
Mayflower Hotel, 51, 79, 105
Mayo, Charles, 63, 65

157

Mayo Clinic, 63, 65
McAdoo, William G., 60
McArthur, Douglas, 120
McArthur, Harry, 127
McCarran, Pat, 89
McCarthy, Joseph R., 131
McClellan, John J., 8
McGraw, James H., Jr., 124
McKaughan, E. E., 96
McKay, David O., 66, 67
McKay, K. Gunn, 150
McKay, Thomas E., 15, 19
McKinney, Frank E., 113, 114, 137
McLaughlin, Frank Y., 61
McQuesten, Roseanna, 89
Meal, Billy, 34
Merrill, Ambrose, 21
Morari, Sam, 26
Morgan, Dale, 60
Morgan, Tom, 82, 90, 96, 101
Mormons (settlement), 1
Mormon Battalion, 6
Moss, Frank E., 149, 150
Moyle, James H., 4
Mt. Pleasant, Utah, 11
Mt. Pleasant Bank, 18
Murray, George D., 81

Nader, Ralph, 149
National Broadcasting Company (NBC), 123, 124
National Safety Council, 79
National Security Act, 100
National Youth Administration, 67, 80
Navarro, Armando, 150
Nelsen, Clarence, 42
Nelson, J. Bert, 140
New Deal, 40, 82, 90, 144
Nibley, Elizabeth Hinckley, 29, 37, 51–53, 107
Nibley, Preston P., 107
Noble, Edward J., 71, 75, 78, 87, 117, 118, 124–26, 135, 136, 139

Oakley, Bert, 90
O'Brian, Robert, 138
Ogden Airport, 58
Ogden, Utah, 33
Ogden Savings Bank, 17
Ogden State Bank, 32, 36, 37
Office of Contract Settlement, 106, 110–17, 121, 122
O'Rourke, Tex, 128

Packard Automobile Company, 25
Paley, William S., 136
Parker, Jake, 33, 44
Patterson, Robert, 113, 114
Pearl Harbor, 93, 123
Pearson, Drew, 130
Pericles, 140
Perkins, Frances, 63
Perry, Harmon, 58
Peterson, William, 49
Polygamy, 6
Porter, Paul, 138, 143
Potomac River, 74
Provo, Utah, 1
Public Works Administration, 45
Putnam, Roger L., 114, 117

Question Club, 26

Radio Corporation of America (RCA), 123, 124
Rampton, Calvin L., 144
Randolph Field, 79
Rankin, Weston, 114
Ray, Paul, 24
Ray, Will, 24
Rayburn, Sam, 132–34
Reconstruction Finance Corporation, 40, 99, 100, 108
Relief Administration Congress, 44
Riddell, James, 138, 139
Romney, George, 147
Roosevelt, Eleanor, 55, 56, 92
Roosevelt, Franklin D., 35, 40–43, 47, 52, 54–57, 63, 65, 68, 70,

72, 73, 75, 78, 79, 83, 86, 93, 106, 107, 109-11, 119, 132, 144
Root, Elihu, 24
Rose, H. Chapman, 114, 117, 119
Rossi, Angelo J., 63, 64
Rushmer, John, 36, 37
Ryan, Oswald, 71

Salt Lake Airport, 58
Salt Lake City, Utah, 1
San Francisco Strike, 62, 63
Scott, Ruth, 150
Seely-Hinckley Automobile Company, 24
Seely, John H., 11-14, 21
Seely, Leonard, 24
Seely, Margaret, 11, 13, 24
Separation of church and state, 3
Shaw, George Bernard, 151
Showaker, Mildred, 44
Simpson, Henry L., 95
Sinatra, Frank, 137
Smith, Al, 22
Smith, Edward B., 114
Smith, Homer, 93
Smith, Rufus D., 83
Smoot, Annie K., 6
Smoot-Hawley Tariff Act, 12
Smoot, Reed, 2, 3, 6, 10, 12, 34
Social Security Program (Mormon), 66
Somervell, Brehon, 115
Sorenson, Perry, 144
Sperry Corporation, 82, 90, 92, 96, 99, 101-6, 111, 116
Sperry, Elmer A., 102
Stephens, Harold H., 71
Steward, J. Harold, 113, 114
Stockdale, William, 30
Stock market crash, 33, 39, 56, 59
Stoddard, Earl, 18
Stoddard, Elmer, 18
Surplus Property Act, 116

Taft, William Howard, 12

Taishoff, Sal, 137
Taitel, Martin, 144
Taylor, Les, 30
Templehof Feld, 72
Thatcher, Paul, 34
Thomas, Danny, 137
Thomas, Elbert D., 4
Thomas, John F., 114
Thomas, Norman, 22
Thomas, T. E., 36, 37
Thompson, Robert, 18, 19
Thurman, Samuel, 145
Tiffany, Kenneth C., 114
Tithing script, 5
Tolson, Clyde, 82
Trez, Oliver, 138
Truman, Bess, 120, 121
Truman, Harry S., 68, 100, 119-21, 145
Tugwell, Rex, 35
Tunney, John V., 147

United Paramount Theatres, 136-38
Universal Broadcasting Company, 125
University of Utah, 34, 53, 84, 144, 145
Utah National Bank, 17, 18
Utah Pacific Airways Aviation Company, 32, 36, 72, 80
Utah Power and Light Company, 21
Utah Relief Organization, 44
Utah State Agriculture College, 49, 84, 141, 145-48, 150
Utah State Institute of Fine Arts, 59
Utah Writers Project, 59, 60
Utility Holding Company Act, 55

Valentine, Hyrum, 19
Volunteer Relief Committee, 38, 39

159

Waldorf Astoria, 120
Wallace, Henry, 119
Wallace, William, 50
Warren, Lindsay C., 115
War Training Service, 93, 96
Washington National Airport, 73–77
Water Conservation and Development Program, 49, 50
Welsh ponies, 142, 143
Westbrook, Lawrence, 61
Wiener, Walter, F., 114
Wilkins, Ernest K., 82
Williams, Aubrey, 63, 68
Williams, J. D., 146, 148, 150
Womans Trade Union League, 56

Wood, Ben D., 80, 96, 98
Wood, Phyllis, 128
Woods, Mark, 125, 136
Works Progress Administration (WPA), 35, 53, 56, 58–60, 62, 63, 65–69, 74, 90, 93, 108
World War I, 27, 28
World War II, 83, 85, 91, 108
Wright, Orville, 71, 75
Wright, Roscoe, 89
Wright, Wilbur, 71, 75

Yellowstone Park, 32, 33
Yerba Buena Island, 60
Young, Brigham, 1, 2, 7